TOP 10
BANGKOK

RON EMMONS

EYEWITNESS TRAVEL

Left **Wat Mahathat** Center **Oriental Spa** Right **Murals, Buddhaisawan Chapel**

LONDON, NEW YORK,
MELBOURNE, MUNICH AND DELHI
www.dk.com

Printed and bound in China by
Leo Paper Products Ltd.

First American Edition, 2008
14 15 16 17 10 9 8 7 6 5 4 3 2 1

Published in the United States by
Dorling Kindersley Limited, 345 Hudson Street,
New York, New York 10014

**Copyright 2008, 2014 © Dorling
Kindersley Limited, London**

Reprinted with revisions 2010, 2012, 2014

A catalog record for this book is available from the
Library of Congress.

ISSN 1479-344X
ISBN 978 1 46541 043 6

Within each Top 10 list in this book, no hierarchy of
quality or popularity is implied. All 10 are, in the
editor's opinion, of roughly equal merit.

Floors are referred to throughout in accordance
with American usage; ie the "first floor" is
at ground level.

MIX
Paper from
responsible sources
FSC™ C018179
www.fsc.org

Contents

Bangkok's Top 10

The information in this DK Eyewitness Top 10 Travel Guide is checked regularly.
Every effort has been made to ensure that this book is as up-to-date as possible at the time of
going to press. Some details, however, such as telephone numbers, opening hours, prices,
gallery hanging arrangements and travel information are liable to change. The publishers
cannot accept responsibility for any consequences arising from the use of this book, nor for
any material on third party websites, and cannot guarantee that any website address in this
book will be a suitable source of travel information. We value the views and suggestions of
our readers very highly. Please write to: Publisher, DK Eyewitness Travel Guides, Dorling
Kindersley, 80 Strand, London WC2R 0RL, UK, or email: travelguides@dk.com.

Left **Crafts, Chatuchak Weekend Market** Center **Dream World** Right **Black Swan pub**

Left **Ton Kem Market** Right **Wat Phra Kaeo**

Key to abbreviations
Adm *admission charge* **extn.** *extension*

BANGKOK'S TOP 10

BANGKOK'S TOP 10

TOP10 Bangkok's Highlights

Beguiling and bewildering, subtle and brash, spiritual and sensual, Bangkok is one of Asia's most intriguing cities. Its glittering temples and museums overflow with sumptuous art, and an exploration of the city's canals and markets reveals the locals' hospitable nature. Shopping for bargains, dining out, and reveling in the vibrant nightlife should feature high on everyone's itinerary.

1 Grand Palace and Wat Phra Kaeo
This dazzling complex is the pinnacle of perfection in Thai religious art and architecture. An unmissable sight *(see pp8–11)*.

2 National Museum
One of the largest museums in Asia, the National Museum displays priceless exhibits including intricate works of art that clearly document the long and eventful history of Thailand *(see pp12–13)*.

3 Wat Pho
Bangkok's oldest and biggest temple, and formerly a center for public education, Wat Pho houses a massive Reclining Buddha and a school of Thai massage *(see pp14–15)*.

4 Bangkok's Canals
Boats were once the city's main mode of transport. Tour the canals west of the Chao Phraya River to glimpse a vanishing lifestyle *(see pp16–17)*.

5 Dusit Park
Seeming a world away from Bangkok's bustle, this tranquil park, studded with royal residences and government offices, is ideal for a peaceful stroll and learning about the Thai monarchy *(see pp18–19)*.

Preceding pages **Demon figures supporting the *chedi* (stupa), Royal Pantheon, Wat Phra Kaeo**

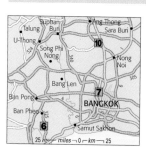

Damnoen Saduak Floating Market

Though designed for tourists, the colorful sights, aromatic smells, and cheerful banter of vendors make a visit to this floating market a delightful experience *(see pp20–21)*.

Chatuchak Weekend Market

Bangkok's biggest market is a must-see, for the chance to pick up a unique souvenir and feel the pulse of Thai culture in the maze of stalls *(see pp22–3)*.

Jim Thompson's House

Assembled by the man who made Thai silk world-famous, this complex of traditional houses is a fine example of Thai teak architecture. The main house remains as it was during the days of Jim Thompson and the other buildings display items from his art collection *(see pp24–5)*.

Ayutthaya

The ancient city of Ayutthaya is easily visited in a day. Its huge, crumbling *chedi* (stupas) and blissful Buddha images give an idea of the splendor of this former capital *(see pp28–31)*.

Wat Arun

With its five distinctive *prang* (towers), which are often used as a logo of the city, this temple played an important historical role in the development of Bangkok and remains one of its most attractive sights *(see pp26–7)*.

Grand Palace and Wat Phra Kaeo

In 1782, Rama I (r.1782–1809) established the capital in Bangkok, where he built Wat Phra Kaeo to house the country's most precious Buddha image. In 1784, he had the Grand Palace built, which became the home of the royal family. No king has resided here since the early 20th century, but the complex is a stunning display of Thai art and architecture and a truly memorable sight.

Amarin Winichai Hall

⊘ Modest dress is essential; no sandals, shorts, or sleeveless shirts allowed.

Visit in the morning to avoid the afternoon heat. Wear a hat or carry an umbrella to protect yourself from the sun. It is usually cooler inside the cloisters.

Keep your ticket for free entry (use within one week) to Vimanmek Palace (see p18).

◗ Carry water, as the only café is at the end of the tour, next to the Dusit Throne Hall.

- Na Phra Lan Road
- Map B4
- (02) 623 5500
- AC bus 503, 508, 512
- Open 8:30am–4:30pm daily
- Adm B500

Top 10 Features

1. Wat Phra Kaeo
2. Siwalai Gardens
3. Amarin Winichai Hall
4. Phaisan Thaksin Hall
5. Chakraphat Phiman Hall
6. Inner Palace
7. Chakri Maha Prasat
8. Aphonphimok Pavilion
9. Dusit Throne Hall
10. Wat Phra Kaeo Museum

Wat Phra Kaeo
Serving as the royal chapel of the Grand Palace, this dazzling complex *(right)* never fails to impress first-time visitors with its slender *chedi* (stupas), glittering mosaics, and other-worldly creatures, such as the fearsome *yaksha* (giants) that stand guard by the gates. The *wat* (temple) is Thailand's holiest shrine, but unlike other Thai temples, there are no resident monks here *(see pp10–11)*.

Siwalai Gardens
These well-kept, picturesque gardens *(below)* were once used for official receptions. Within the gardens are two buildings. The Neo-Classical Boromphiman Mansion, was built by Rama V *(see p34)* for the Crown Prince (later Rama VI), and now serves as a guesthouse for visiting dignitaries. The Phra Buddha Ratana Sathan was built as a personal chapel by Rama IV *(see p34)*.

Amarin Winichai Hall
This was one of the first buildings of the palace complex to be completed, and was originally used as an audience hall for foreign guests. Inside, the hall has colorful murals and Rama I's boat-shaped Busabok Mala Throne surmounted by a nine-tiered white canopy. Today the hall is used for state cermonies and is open to the public on weekdays.

Phaisan Thaksin Hall

This hall *(left)* is not open to the public and is used only for coronations. It contains the Coronation Chair and the tutelary deity, Phra Siam Thewathirat.

Dusit Throne Hall

For many, this building *(below)* is the site's crowning glory, featuring a four-tiered roof and Rama I's teak throne.

Wat Phra Kaeo Museum

This museum displays a treasure trove of artifacts salvaged from restoration of the palace, including costumes of the Emerald Buddha *(see p11)*.

Chakraphat Phiman Hall

Closed to the public, this hall was the residence of the first three kings of the Chakri dynasty *(see p34)*. It consists of a royal bedchamber and a reception chamber housing the regalia and accoutrements of kingship.

Inner Palace

Until the time of Rama VII (r.1925–35), the Inner Palace was inhabited solely by women. All males except the king were forbidden entry. Still closed to the public, it is now a school for girls from prominent families.

Chakri Maha Prasat

Occupying center stage in the Grand Palace is the Chakri throne hall *(right)*. Built by Rama V in 1882, it is a fusion of Western and Thai architectural styles. The ashes of Chakri kings are housed here.

Aphonphimok Pavilion

This small but attractive pavilion was built by Rama IV as a royal changing room prior to audiences in the adjacent Dusit Throne Hall. Its multi-tiered roof and elaborate decoration are hallmarks of classic Thai design.

Entering and Getting Around the Complex

All visitors enter by the gate on Na Phra Lan Road, where anyone inappropriately dressed is required to hire clothes. At the ticket office it is possible to rent an audio-tape or hire a guide to explain the significance of the sights. Visitors usually walk clockwise around Wat Phra Kaeo before exploring the rest of the Grand Palace. It takes at least two hours to walk around the site.

Left *Ramakien* murals Center Royal Pantheon Right Model of Angkor Wat

TOP 10 Wat Phra Kaeo

1 Ramakien Murals
Stretching over half a mile (1 km) along the cloister walls of the temple, the *Ramakien* murals portray scenes from the Hindu epic, *Ramayana*, in 178 panels of intricate detail and vibrant color.

2 Phra Si Rattana Chedi
This glittering, cone-shaped *chedi* (stupa) is one of the most photographed features of Wat Phra Kaeo. Built of gold tiles in the Sri Lankan style, it stands majestically on the upper terrace beside the Phra Mondop.

3 Phra Mondop
This building towers almost as high as the Phra Si Rattana Chedi and is a repository for sacred Buddhist texts. Its deep-green mosaics are the perfect backdrop for the seated stone Buddhas at each corner.

4 Royal Pantheon
The pantheon enshrines life-size statues of the past rulers of the Chakri dynasty *(see p34)* and completes the trio of tall buildings on the upper terrace.

5 Model of Angkor Wat
Tucked away behind the Phra Mondop, this model of Angkor Wat was installed by Rama IV *(see p34)*, when Cambodia was under Thai rule.

6 Wihan Yot
Often called "the porcelain *wihan*", this delicately adorned prayer hall stands in the center of the north terrace and contains a number of Buddha images.

Wihan Yot

7 Hor Phra Nak and Ho Phra Monthien Tham
Flanking the Wihan Yot on the north terrace are the Hor Phra Nak, a royal mausoleum with urns that hold the ashes of members of the royal family, and the Ho Phra Monthien Tham, a library that has particularly fine doors inlaid with mother-of-pearl.

8 The Bot
The most-visited building in the temple grounds is the *bot* (ordination hall), which contains the much-venerated Emerald Buddha. The interior walls are smothered with murals, the altar is richly decorated, and the scent of incense is thick as Thais pay respect to the image that is the country's talisman.

The dazzling golden Phra Si Rattana Chedi

The Royal Pantheon is open to the public only on Chakri Day (April 6) each year

9 The Emerald Buddha

Made of jadeite rather than emerald, the most sacred image in the kingdom is just 26 inches (66 cm) tall. Thought to have been crafted in Sri Lanka, it was housed in Chiang Rai, Lampang, and Laos before Rama I (r.1782–1809) brought it to Bangkok.

Chapel of Gandahara Buddha

10 Chapel of Gandahara Buddha

In the southeast corner of the temple compound stands a small chapel with beautifully painted doors. Usually locked, it contains an image, used in the Royal Ploughing Ceremony *(see p48)* of the Buddha calling down the rains.

Top 10 Thai Mythical Creatures

1. Naga – serpent-like protector of the Buddha
2. Singha – lion-like temple guardian
3. Yaksha – giant
4. Garuda – half-man, half-bird
5. Erawan – three-headed elephant
6. Kinnari – half-woman, half-bird
7. Aponsi – half-woman, half-lion
8. Hongsa – swan-like figure
9. Makara – part crocodile, part elephant, part serpent
10. Mom – dragon-like temple guardian

Mythical Creatures in Thai Temples

Before visitors get to see the beautifully crafted Buddha images that adorn the wihan *and* bot *of any Thai temple compound, including Wat Phra Kaeo, they have to pass a panoply of fearsome creatures that act as temple guardians. Most of these beings are from the legendary Himaphan Forest, a kind of Buddhist Shangri-La somewhere in the Himalayan Mountains. These include* singha, *lion-like figures that sit atop gateposts, and* yaksha, *grimacing giants with brightly colored faces that tower above entrances to the compound. The steps leading up to the* wihan *and* bot *are usually flanked by multi-headed* naga, *serpents that according to legend sheltered the Buddha from a storm while he was meditating. Some temple balustrades depict* makara, *aquatic monsters that symbolize rainfall, devouring the* naga. *The* hongsa, a *swan-like entity, is often seen perched on the apex of a temple roof. The* kinnari – *half-woman, half-bird – is seen in wall niches or skipping down temple eaves.*

Intricate craftsmanship displayed on the *bot* at Wat Phra Kaeo

TOP10 National Museum

Thailand's premier museum offers a great introduction to Thai history. Inside, the Buddhaisawan Chapel is one of the country's most precious treasures, as is the Phra Sihing Buddha image it houses. Other highlights include well-preserved fragments of Dvaravati and Srivajaya statues, as well as the Ramkhamhaeng inscription.

Detail of a chariot, Royal Funeral Chariots Gallery

To make better sense of the museum, join the free guided tour at 9:30am either on Wednesdays or on Thursdays.

The museum covers a big area, but there are seats in shaded corners between galleries where you can take a break.

There is a kiosk just inside the entrance selling cold drinks, ice creams, and snacks.

- Na Phra That Road
- Map B3
- (02) 224 1333
- Bus 508, 511, 512
- Open 9am–4pm Wed–Sun
- Adm B50
- www.nationalmuseums.finearts.go.th/thaimuseum_eng/bangkok/service.htm

Top 10 Features

1. Buddhaisawan Chapel
2. Phra Sihing Buddha Image
3. Dvaravati Wheel of Law
4. Gallery of Thai History
5. Lanna Art
6. Sukhothai Art
7. Red House
8. Royal Funeral Chariots Gallery
9. Rattanakosin Art
10. Ayutthayan Art

1 Buddhaisawan Chapel

This beautiful Thai temple was built in 1787 for the Second King and now sits at the heart of the National Museum complex. Its rich murals, polished floors, gilt Buddha images, and hushed atmosphere make it a special place *(above)*.

2 Phra Sihing Buddha Image

One of three such images claiming to be the original, this small but superbly crafted Sukhothai-style sculpture sits on a pedestal in the Buddhaisawan Chapel *(above)* and is bathed in a golden glow.

3 Dvaravati Wheel of Law

Dvaravati art flourished from the 6th to the 9th centuries, and this 8th-century stone wheel set above a deer is an excellent example *(below)*. Located on the second floor of the south wing, it represents the Buddha's first sermon in Sarnath, India.

4 Gallery of Thai History

The first gallery *(below)* of the museum gives an overview of Thai history, ranging from pre-history to the modern era. It includes some priceless objects, such as the Ramkhamhaeng Stone, inscribed with the earliest extant example of the Thai script.

During the Songkran festival every year the Phra Sihing Buddha image is paraded around Sanam Luang see p48

Sukhothai Art
6 Sukhothai art is often considered to be the apex of Thai artistic achievement, and the flowing lines of walking and sitting Buddha images in the museum fully support this notion *(below)*.

Lanna Art
5 Several small Buddha images from the Lanna period, 13th–16th centuries, are on display here *(above)*.

Red House
7 A fine example of an Ayutthaya-style teak house, the Red House *(above)* was originally the home of Rama I's (r.1782–1809) older sister, Sri Suriyen. It has a multi-tiered roof decorated with beautiful carvings, and the interior contains some antique royal furnishings.

Royal Funeral Chariots Gallery
8 The elaborately decorated carriages in this gallery give an idea of the pomp and ceremony that accompany royal funerals. Each of the gilded teak carriages weighs several tons and needs hundreds of men to pull them.

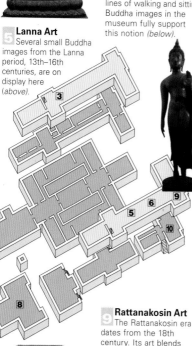

Rattanakosin Art
9 The Rattanakosin era dates from the 18th century. Its art blends Western influences with traditional Thai art. The last gallery in the north wing of the museum displays examples of Rattanakosin paintings and furnishings *(below)*.

Key

▩	1st Floor
▨	2nd Floor

Origin of the National Museum

The site on which the National Museum now stands was once the home of the Second King of Thailand. It was built for Rama I's viceroy, Prince Wang Na, in 1782. However, a century later, in 1887, Rama V decided to abolish the office of the Second King and turned the building into the country's first museum so that the people in his kingdom could appreciate their rich cultural heritage.

Ayutthayan Art
10 Huge, serene Buddha heads, as well as scripture cabinets *(above)* adorned with scenes of Ayutthaya in its heyday, are displayed in the Ayutthayan gallery.

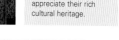

10 Wat Pho

Bangkok's oldest and largest temple, Wat Pho has the country's longest Reclining Buddha. Built in the 16th century and reconstructed by Rama I (r.1782–1809), it is a typical Thai temple, with resident monks, a school, massage pavilions, and a generally lived-in feel. Around the grounds are statues and chedi (stupas) glittering with mosaics.

Statues of hermits on the miniature mountains

Great Chedi, Wat Pho

⊘ Most visitors enter the compound from Thanon Thai Wang, right next to the Reclining Buddha. However, the southern entrance on Soi Chetupon allows you to appreciate the rest of the compound in comparative peace before finally arriving at the temple's most popular highlight.

⊜ Several basic food shops line the western border of the temple, including Rub Aroon, which serves refreshing fruit juices and coffees.

- Soi Chetuphon
- Map B5
- (02) 226 0335
- AC bus 503, 508, 512
- Open 8am–6pm daily
- Adm B100
- www.watpho.com

Top 10 Features

1. Reclining Buddha
2. Feet of Reclining Buddha
3. Traditional Massage
4. Medicine Pavilion
5. The Bot
6. Miniature Mountains
7. Monks and Their Guti
8. Schoolkids and Classrooms
9. Great Chedi
10. Farang Guards

1 Reclining Buddha
The 151-ft (46-m) long, 50-ft (15-m) high Reclining Buddha, made of brick, plaster, and gold leaf, fills the *wihan* (assembly hall) in the northwest corner of the temple compound. Visitors are guided first past the face, with its serene expression, and then to the feet, which are studded with mother-of-pearl inlay.

2 Feet of Reclining Buddha
The soles of the feet of the Reclining Buddha are inlaid with 108 *lakshana*, or auspicious images that identify the true Buddha. Crafted in shimmering mother-of-pearl, these images are a dazzling work of art *(below)*.

3 Traditional Massage
Wat Pho is known as a center for traditional medicine and since the 1960s has run what is considered the best massage school in Thailand. Highly trained masseurs are on hand to relieve visitors of their aches and pains. The school also offers 10- or 15-day massage courses, which are taught in both Thai and English.

Medicine Pavilion
Located in the heart of the complex, the Medicine Pavilion has stone tablets *(above)* indicating the pressure points on the body that should be used during traditional Thai massage.

The Bot
This ordination hall is Wat Pho's largest building, and contains a large bronze image of a meditating Buddha *(below)*, in the base of which are the ashes of Rama I.

Miniature Mountains
Scattered around the complex are several man-made mounds on which are statues of hermits in unusual postures. These are intended to teach people the healing positions for the body.

Monks and Their Guti
Away from the *wihan* housing the Reclining Buddha, visitors might encounter monks who work at the temple. They live in *guti* (small, simple rooms) in a compound to the south of the temple.

Schoolkids and Classrooms
In Wat Pho, as in many Thai temples, there is a school for children. At playtime, the temple compound echoes with their excited screams. Some may even try a few words of English on visitors.

Farang Guards
Adding a whimsical touch to this temple of learning are huge stone caricatures of Westerners, *farang* in Thai, wearing top hats *(right)*. These guards stand beside the gateways to the inner courtyard of the temple. The statues arrived as ballast on trade ships returning from China.

Great Chedi
There are about 100 *chedi* in the grounds of Wat Pho *(above)*, but the four most important, situated in the western courtyard, are the Great Chedi, which honor the first four kings of the Chakri dynasty *(see p34)*. The *chedi* are decorated with porcelain mosaic.

Reclining Buddhas
To a person unfamiliar with Buddhism, a Reclining Buddha appears to be relaxing or even sleeping, but this interpretation could not be farther from the truth. While other images of him standing, sitting, or walking show aspects of his quest to attain Enlightenment, a Reclining Buddha symbolizes his arrival at Nirvana, a state of all-knowing awareness that is the complete antithesis of relaxation or sleep.

 The Medicine Pavilion now functions as a souvenir shop for tourists

⒑ Bangkok's Canals

In the 19th century, Bangkok was known as the "Venice of the East," since all transportation was by canal. Today, most of the canals to the east of the Chao Phraya River have been filled in to create new roads. However, the area to the west remains much as it was in the 19th century, with a network of waterways spreading out into the countryside. Here, visitors can get a taste of traditional canalside life and visit a few attractions such as Wat Arun and the Royal Barge Museum along the way.

Traditional Thai house

🕐 To tour the canals, either hire a longtail boat (about B800–1000 per hour) from any riverside pier, join an organized tour on a larger boat, or take the river bus to Nonthaburi *(see box)*.

📍 Organized tours usually provide refreshments for passengers or make a scheduled stop where they can buy drinks and snacks from floating vendors.

• Chao Phraya River: Map B5
• Khlong Bangkok Noi: Map A2
• Khlong Bangkok Yai: Map B6
• Khlong Mon: Map A5

Top 10 Features

1. Chao Phraya – River of Kings
2. Boats
3. Royal Barge Museum
4. Wat Arun
5. Traditional Thai Houses
6. Canalside Activities
7. Floating Vendors
8. Khlong Bangkok Yai
9. Khlong Bangkok Noi
10. Khlong Mon

¹ Chao Phraya – River of Kings

Without the Chao Phraya River, there would be no Bangkok. Named for the founder of the Chakri dynasty, Chao Phraya Chakri *(see p34)*, the river has always been the lifeblood of the nation, providing an aquatic highway for a mesmerizing variety of boats.

² Boats

The river carries such a wide range of vessels that it is great fun just to sit at a riverside café and watch the pageant flow. Huge barges chug downstream, while small ferries *(above)* nip from bank to bank, and longtail boats with bright awnings roar past.

³ Royal Barge Museum

This museum *(see p89)* contains a fabulous display of ornamented royal barges *(below)*, which are about 165 ft (50 m) long. Also on display are dioramas of robes worn by royal rowers, and information on the use of the barges, which is limited to royal processions on the river.

Wat Arun
4 Established by King Rama I, Wat Arun *(left)* is known as the Temple of the Dawn. Its main features are the five *prang* (towers) which are encrusted with colorful pieces of porcelain *(see pp26–7)*.

Traditional Thai Houses
5 Traditional Thai houses line the canals to the west of the Chao Phraya River. Set on stilts to avoid flooding, they usually have an open veranda and steeply pitched roofs to keep them cool.

Canalside Activities
6 A canal trip allows visitors to get a glimpse of everyday Thai life as people cook and chat on the riverbanks, and children swim in the canal.

Floating Vendors
7 Authentic floating vendors are rare today, but most tour boats make a scheduled stop where a local comes paddling by, offering cold drinks, straw hats, postcards, and smiles for the camera.

Khlong Bangkok Noi
9 Though it is now termed a *khlong*, or canal, this waterway was once the main channel of the Chao Phraya River. Near its entrance is the Royal Barge Museum and a little farther on is Wat Suwannaram which has some rich murals.

Khlong Mon
10 Branching off from the Chao Phraya River just north of Wat Arun, this canal *(right)* leads to an orchid farm where visitors step ashore for a look around before continuing to explore the canal.

Khlong Bangkok Yai
8 This canal is very popular with tour boats as it passes several temples, including Wat Kalayanamit, which has a huge Buddha image, and Wat Pak Nam, famous for its amulets. Many boats also stop at a snake farm and the floating market along Khlong Dao Khanong.

Riding the Chao Phraya Express
The cheapest way to explore Bangkok's waterways is by riding the Chao Phraya Express, a river bus which runs between Sathorn Pier *(Map M6)* and Phra Athit Pier *(Map B2)*. The complete journey takes around 75 minutes, passing by several historical sights, such as the Church of Santa Cruz *(see p92)*, Wat Arun, Wat Phra Kaeo *(see pp8–11)*, and Wat Rakhang *(see p92)*.

TOP 10 Dusit Park

Sometimes referred to as the New Royal City, Dusit is home to several royal residences and government offices. Dusit Park was created by Rama V (r.1868–1910) in an attempt to emulate parks that he had seen on visits to Europe. The green and shady paths are a pleasure to walk along, with many interesting sights on offer.

Cloth and Silk Museum, Dusit Park

🍴 There is a café selling drinks and snacks at the entrance to Vimanmek Palace, but it is a good idea to carry water with you as it can be thirsty work visiting all the park's attractions.

- Map E1
- (02) 628 6300
- Bus 510 and 70
- Vimanmek Palace: open 9am–3:15pm Tue–Sun; adm B100 (includes entry to all museums) or free with Grand Palace ticket; guided tours every half hour; last tour 3:15pm; www.vimanmek.com
- Ananta Samakhom Throne Hall: open 9:30am–4pm daily
- SUPPORT Museum: open 9:30am–4pm daily
- Photographic Museum: open 9:30am–4pm daily
- Royal Elephant Museum: open 9am–4pm daily
- Old Clock Museum: open 9:30am–4pm daily
- Ancient Textile Museum: open 9:30am–4pm daily

Top 10 Features

1. Vimanmek Palace
2. Royal Plaza
3. Ananta Samakhom Throne Hall
4. Abhisek Dusit Throne Hall/ SUPPORT Museum
5. Photographic Museum
6. Royal Elephant Museum
7. Old Clock Museum
8. Ancient Textile Museum
9. Lakeside Pavilion
10. Dusit Zoo

Vimanmek Palace

Possibly the world's largest teak building *(right)*, this palace was the home of Rama V *(see p34)* in the early 20th century and contains a huge collection of royal artifacts. Visitors can join a guided tour to see 30 of its 72 rooms.

Royal Plaza

At the entrance to Dusit Park is this large open area dominated by an equestrian statue of Rama V who designed the park. Each year on December 5, the present king's birthday, the spectacular Trooping of the Colors is held here.

Ananta Samakhom Throne Hall

Built in Renaissance style and capped with a huge dome, this gray marble throne hall *(above)* is the largest building in Dusit Park. It houses the Art of the Kingdom exhibition.

Abhisek Dusit Throne Hall/ SUPPORT Museum

This attractive building is an unusual mixture of Victorian, Islamic, and Thai styles, with some delightful timber latticework around the entrance *(left)*. It contains the SUPPORT Museum, which features jewelry, silk, and wicker items produced by a charity foundation set up by Queen Sirikit to promote traditional crafts. The throne hall is used for royal receptions.

Bangkok's Top 10

6 Royal Elephant Museum

The former stables of the king's white elephants house this museum *(left)*, which features pachyderm paraphernalia such as howdahs, sacred ropes, and mahouts' amulets. There are photos of the king's white elephants, as well as a model of a current favorite. White elephants in Thailand all belong to the king.

5 Photographic Museum

Rama IX *(see box)* is a keen and accomplished photographer and examples of his work are on display here.

7 Old Clock Museum

The splendid table, wall, and grandfather clocks on display here were commissioned or acquired by kings Rama V and Rama IX on their trips to Europe *(below)*.

8 Ancient Textile Museum

This museum displays a range of fabrics favored by the court of Rama V, such as Shanghai brocade silk, gold brocade cloth, and satin. There are also textiles produced by Queen Sirikit's SUPPORT Foundation on display here.

10 Dusit Zoo

Covering 47 acres (19 hectares) and housing over 300 mammals, 300 reptiles, and 1,000 birds in its grounds, this is one of Asia's better zoos. Some varieties of tropical flora are still cultivated here, originally the private botanical gardens of Rama V. The lawns, lakes, and wooded glades are ideal for relaxing strolls. At weekends it gets crowded with families wandering, snacking, and taking boat rides *(see p46)*.

9 Lakeside Pavilion

Overlooking a tranquil stretch of water is a delightful lakeside pavilion. Decorated with ornate carvings, it is occasionally used for performances of Thai dancing *(below)*.

The Thai Royal Family

Rama IX *(see p35)* is the world's longest reigning monarch, having acceded to the throne in 1946. He has initiated many projects to improve the lives of his people. Although Thai monarchs have always been treated like demigods, it is remarkable in this modern era to see the devotion the Thais have for their king.

🔟 Damnoen Saduak Floating Market

Today, the many waterways of Bangkok's once extensive canal network have been filled up to make new roads, but for visitors the image of floating vendors in traditional dress remains quintessentially Thai. So each morning, vendors and tourists alike descend on Damnoen Saduak to re-enact scenes from an idealized past. Visitors can explore the rural canals, take pictures of colorful boats, and shop for souvenirs.

Traditional costumes of the sampan vendors

🕐 To enjoy the market before busloads of tourists arrive (usually around 9–10am), it is necessary to stay overnight in a local guest house and get out on the canals in the early morning.

🍴 Most guided tours include refreshments, but there are plenty of vendors selling food and drink for independent travelers.

• 62 miles (100 km) SW of Bangkok
• Map S2
• (03) 224 1204
• AC bus 78 from Bangkok's Southern Bus Terminal

Top 10 Features

1. Boats
2. Ton Kem Market
3. Hia Kui Market
4. Khun Pitak Market
5. Fruits
6. Bridge
7. Boat Vendors
8. Fruit Orchards
9. Boat Noodles
10. Souvenirs

1 Boats
Most vendors paddle around in *sampan*, which are simple, square-ended rowing boats that are easily maneuvered and ideal for displaying goods for sale. The tourists, however, are propelled around the canals in longtail boats. These boats can be noisy but offer protection from the elements and can cover a big area in a short time.

2 Ton Kem Market
What is normally referred to as Damnoen Saduak Floating Market actually consists of three separate markets. The biggest of these is Ton Kem Market on Khlong Damnoen Saduak. The market is very popular with both tour groups and vendors, the result being that the canal often gets jammed with boats.

A vendor doing brisk business in a *sampan*

3 Hia Kui Market
A short way south of Ton Kem, Hia Kui market *(below)* is less frequented by tourists and hence has a more authentic feel to it. The banks of the canal are dotted with souvenir shops where some group tours stop for mementos.

4 Khun Pitak Market

Located on a smaller *khlong*, or canal, a little over a mile (2 km) south of Hia Kui, Khun Pitak is the least crowded of the three markets. However it is still a bustling place early in the morning when locals buy their breakfast or fresh produce, including fruits, vegetables, and spices, from the vendors.

5 Fruits

Many of the *sampan* on the canals here sell pomelos, bananas, rose apples, and jackfruit that are freshly picked from local orchards *(above)*.

6 Bridge

Although there are plenty of opportunities for taking pictures while exploring the canals by boat, the classic view of the floating market, thick with vendors and colorful produce, is from the bridge that crosses the canal at Ton Kem market.

7 Boat Vendors

The *sampan* that the vendors paddle along the canals provide no protection from the elements, so most vendors wear a *ngob* – a traditional hat that ingeniously allows for ventilation. Many also wear a collarless denim shirt typical in rural Thailand.

8 Fruit Orchards

To add variety to a visit to the floating market, many tour groups include a visit to an orchard to look at the trees and sample ripe fruit. Some orchards also keep harmless pythons, which tourists can drape round their necks for a souvenir photo.

Other Floating Markets

Damnoen Saduak gets the lion's share of visitors to floating markets, but there are other locations in and around Bangkok where similar markets operate, though some of them only function once a week. These include Amphawa, Tha Kha, Lam Phya, Don Wai, Wat Sai, and Taling Chan. The last two are near the center of Bangkok, but are exclusively for tourists and lack the photogenic nature of the markets at Damnoen Saduak.

9 Boat Noodles

It is a minor miracle that cooks can prepare a tasty bowl of *gooaydteeo rua*, or boat noodles, in a small boat and serve it without spilling a drop *(below)*. These dishes are so popular that noodle shops often display their goods in a boat.

10 Souvenirs

Since busloads of tourists arrive in Damnoen Saduak every morning, it is not surprising to find that many locals operate souvenir stalls on the banks of the canals, selling traditional hats *(above)*, silk purses, carved soaps, and, of course, colorful postcards of the market.

Chatuchak Weekend Market

Chatuchak market, held every Saturday and Sunday, is the biggest market in Thailand. An estimated quarter of a million people visit this veritable shopaholic's paradise each day. The vast site has over 15,000 stalls but products are grouped into sections making it easy to find specific items.

Pretty tropical flowers on display

🕑 Go to Chatuchak in the morning to avoid the worst of the heat in the afternoon. Bargaining is expected and some vendors will reduce their initial prices by half.

Simple maps are handed out free but serious shoppers should pick up Nancy Chandler's map of Bangkok, available at many bookstores and hotels, which includes useful tips about Chatuchak.

🕑 To eat and drink in air-conditioned comfort, head for the Dream Section, where there are several smart restaurants.

• Map T5
• Thanon Phaholyothin
• Skytrain Mo Chit, Subway Chatuchak Park or Kampaeng Phet
• Open 6am–6pm Sat & Sun
• www.chatuchak.org

Top 10 Features

1. Antiques
2. Crafts
3. Clothing and Accessories
4. Home Decor
5. Books
6. Food and Drink Stalls
7. Central Clock Tower
8. Chatuchak Park
9. Plants
10. Artists

Antiques
Located in section 26 of the market, antiques on sale in Chatuchak include furniture, paintings, Buddha images *(right)*, lamps, jewelry, clocks, and carvings. However, take care when considering a purchase, because first of all genuine antiques need documentation for customs clearance, and secondly, Thai craftsmen are highly skilled in creating fakes.

Crafts
Thailand is renowned all over the world for its handicrafts, including woodcarvings, basketware, lacquerware, ceramics, silk, silverware, and musical instruments. Such items can be found in section 8 of the market, where, with a little bit of luck, all the gifts you may need for friends and family can be bought in one go.

Plants on sale, Chatuchak Weekend Market

Clothing and Accessories
Around 5,000 stalls sell either clothes *(below)* or fashion accessories. Most of them are in sections 12, 14, 16, 18, and 20. With rock-bottom prices, these are some of the most popular and crowded sections of the market.

5 Books

Bibliophiles will love section 1 which has remaindered art books stacked beside collectible first editions and back issues of magazines. It is best visited last as the weight of purchases may discourage farther exploration of the market.

4 Home Decor

Items to beautify your home *(above)* can be found in sections 2 to 7. If you wish to buy bulky items, you can ship them home via a number of shipping companies in the market.

6 Food and Drink Stalls

More than 400 food and drink stalls *(above)* are scattered throughout the market. Many of these stalls sell only one dish in which they are experts, so snacking here can be a gourmet experience.

7 Central Clock Tower

The tall clocktower *(above)* in the heart of the market is a useful landmark because it is visible from many areas. If you get lost, head for this clocktower, from where it should be easy to find your way.

9 Plants

In this section of the market you can pick up a young fruit tree or a rose bush, a sweet-smelling jasmine plant or a delicate orchid. They also sell fertilizer, flower pots, and gardening tools.

10 Artists

There is an excellent art market, located in section 7, with small studios producing good-value paintings as well as higher-end pieces of art. Artists can be viewed at work on original pieces, and it is also possible to commission reproductions.

8 Chatuchak Park

If you need a break from the crowds, take a stroll in the adjacent Chatuchak Park, just north of the market. Opened in December 1980, the park has a lot of open space and shaded areas. Running the length of the park is an artificial lake with a number of bridges crossing it. Inside the park is the Hall of Railway Heritage. The large exhibition hall of the museum showcases old steam locomotives and rail carriages. Miniature trains of different sizes are also displayed.

Endangered Species

Unfortunately, Thailand is a major conduit for the sale of endangered species from neighboring countries. Several raids on dealers in Chatuchak Weekend Market have revealed animals being kept in awful conditions, and while casual visitors are never likely to see them, this illegal trade still continues out of sight.

Jim Thompson's House

Jim Thompson, an American who came to Bangkok in 1945, is credited with having revived the Thai art of silk weaving. His traditional Thai house is filled with Southeast Asian antiques, paintings, and sculptures. Surrounded by a lush garden, the compound consists of five other teak houses on stilts which also showcase part of the collection.

Offerings at the Spirit House

🅐 Ignore any touts hanging around near the house who tell you that it is closed; they just want to take you shopping elsewhere so that they can get a commission.

The branch of Jim Thompson Silk that is located on the grounds of the house sells many small items such as ties and purses that make great gifts for friends back home.

🅑 There is an excellent café on the premises that looks out over a tranquil pond and serves a good range of meals and snacks.

• 6 Soi Kasem San 2, Rama 1 Road
• Map P2
• (02) 216 7368
• Skytrain National Stadium
• Open 9am–5pm daily
• Adm B100
• www.jimthompson house.com

Top 10 Features

1. Jataka Paintings
2. Burmese Carvings
3. Master Bedroom
4. Dvaravati Buddha Torso
5. Drawing Room
6. Dining Room
7. Traditional Teak Houses
8. Spirit House
9. Ban Khrua Silk Weavers
10. The Garden

Master Bedroom

With a great view over the garden, the master bedroom *(above)* of the house is decorated with large sculptures, paintings of the *Jataka Tales*, and photographs of Jim Thompson on a bedside table.

Jataka Paintings

Near the entrance of the house are scenes from the *Jataka Tales*, which depict the incarnations of the Buddha. The panels, painted in the early 19th century, still retain their rich colors and detail *(above)*.

Burmese Carvings

These intricate carvings display a high level of artistic ability. Jim Thompson's extensive collection of wooden figures includes images of *Nat (right)*, animist spirits which were incorporated into Buddhism when it developed in Burma.

Dvaravati Buddha Torso

Probably the most significant example of early Asian art at the complex, this headless Buddha torso *(above)*, made of limestone during the Dvaravati period (7th–8th centuries), was found in Lopburi Province. The statue is on display in the garden that surrounds the house.

5 Drawing Room

The centerpiece of the house, this large and airy room looks out onto a terrace and is decorated in rich orange and red colors *(right)*. It houses a 14th-century sandstone head of the Buddha and wooden carvings of Burmese figures set in illuminated alcoves.

6 Dining Room

Like the master bedroom, the dining room also enjoys lovely views of the garden. The room features several items of Ming porcelain as well as some fine paintings. The dining table, which consists of two mahjong tables put together, is laid out for a meal as it might have been during the days of Jim Thompson.

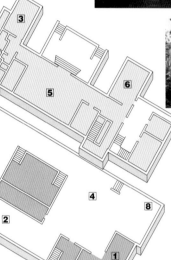

7 Traditional Teak Houses

Their roofs are steeply pitched for ventilation, and the walls lean inward to create a sense of height *(above)*.

Key

▨	1st Floor
▨	2nd Floor

Jim Thompson's Disappearance

On Easter Day, 1967, Jim Thompson went out walking in the Cameron Highlands in Malaysia, and was never seen again. Since he once worked for the Office of Strategic Services (OSS), a predecessor of the CIA, this fuelled suspicion that he was abducted by Vietnamese communists, though others suspect he was hit by a truck and that the driver buried the remains. Since his body was never found, the mystery is likely to stay unsolved.

10 The Garden

Surrounding the house is a garden with cooling pools and dense tropical vegetation *(below)* including flowers, banana plants, and palm trees.

8 Spirit House

Located near the canal, the spirit house generally has offerings of flowers and incense to appease the spirit of the land on which the house stands.

9 Ban Khrua Silk Weavers

Thompson initially chose the location of his house beside Khlong Saen Saep because a silk weavers' community lived at Ban Khrua, on the opposite bank. This made it easy for him to oversee their work.

🔟 Wat Arun

Wat Arun is named for Aruna, the Indian god of dawn, because King Taksin arrived here at sunrise on an October day in 1767 to establish Thonburi as Siam's new capital. With its prominent prang (towers), the temple shows a strong Khmer influence. All the prang are ornamentally encrusted with colorful broken porcelain.

Wat Arun at twilight

Kinnari *in Wat Arun*

○ Wat Arun is undergoing major renovations until fall 2016; parts of the temple complex are likely to be closed to visitors until then.

Although strolling food and drink vendors occasionally visit the temple, there is no permanent café here, so make sure to carry water with you.

○ If you visit in the late afternoon, you can pause for refreshment at a café on the east bank of the river.

- 34 Arun Amarin Road
- Map B5
- (02) 891 1149
- Ferry from Tha Thien Pier
- Open 8am–6pm daily (parts of the temple may be closed and opening times may vary due to renovations being carried out until fall 2016)
- Adm B50
- www.watarun.org

Top 10 Features

1. River View
2. Ceramic Details
3. Central Prang
4. Symbolic Levels
5. Stairs on Central Prang
6. The Bot
7. Chinese Guards
8. Mondop
9. Kinnari
10. Decoration of Minor Prang

River View
It may be called the Temple of Dawn, but the best view of Wat Arun is at sunset from the east bank of the river. There are several cafés and restaurants around Tha Thien from where you can watch the sun slip down behind the soaring *prang (below).*

Ceramic Details
The colorful broken ceramics that cover the *prang* are an ingenious form of 19th-century recycling. In those days, Chinese trading ships carried broken porcelain as ballast, which when offloaded was used to decorate the *prang (center).*

Central Prang
The central *prang (below)* was extended to its current height of 266 ft (81 m) by Rama III (r.1824–51) and represents Mount Meru, the abode of the gods in Hindu-Buddhist cosmology. It is topped with a thunderbolt, the weapon of the god Indra, who also features in niches on the *prang* riding the three-headed elephant Erawan.

Symbolic Levels

The central *prang* has three symbolic levels. The base stands for *Traiphum*, all realms of existence in the Buddhist universe; the middle section represents the *Tavatimsa*, where all desires are gratified; the top denotes *Devaphum*, six heavens within seven realms of happiness.

Stairs on Central Prang

The steep and narrow stairs up the central *prang* represent the difficulties humans face when trying to attain a higher level of enlightenment. They lead up to a narrow terrace that offers a sweeping view, but the upper stairway is often closed.

The Bot

The Buddha image in the *bot* (ordination hall) was apparently molded by Rama II (r.1809–24) himself, and his ashes are buried in the base of the statue *(above)*. The murals were created during the reign of Rama V *(see p34)*. The entrance is guarded by two giants.

Chinese Guards

Eight sets of steps lead up to the first terrace, and each set is guarded by Chinese figures that may have arrived as ballast on ships along with the porcelain. There are also statues of many mythical creatures scattered on the terrace.

Kinnari

Tucked away in small coves on the second level of the central prang are *kinnari*, mythical creatures that are half-bird, half-woman. Renowned for their singing, dancing, and poetry, *kinnari* are just one of the mythical creatures from the Himaphan Forest at the base of Mount Meru.

Mondop

Between each of the four corner *prang* is an elaborately decorated *mondop* (altar). Each holds a Buddha statue at key stages of his life – birth (north), meditation (east), preaching his first sermon (south), and entering Nirvana (west).

Decoration of Minor Prang

Representing the four great seas, these smaller *prang* are also decorated with colorful ceramics. Each *prang*, supported by demons and monkeys, has a niche with a statue of Phra Pai, god of wind, on a white horse *(right)*.

The Rise and Fall of King Taksin

Taksin the Great (r.1768–82) became one of Siam's most successful warrior kings. He rallied factions of Siamese troops after the fall of Ayutthaya, and waged wars with Cambodia, Laos, and the Malays. By the 1770s he had expanded Siam to its largest-ever extent. But success went to his head and he was eventually ousted in a coup and was executed by being clubbed to death in a velvet sack so that royal blood would not touch the ground.

🔟 Ayutthaya

From the 14th century onwards, Ayutthaya was the capital of an independent kingdom until the city was sacked by the Burmese in 1767. It was never re-inhabited. Today, Ayutthaya is a UNESCO World Heritage Site and its ruins give a sense of the city's former size and glory as well as offering an insight into Thailand's cultural heritage.

Wat Phra Ram

🅲 Some tour agencies include a boat trip either to or from Ayutthaya, the ideal way to approach the historic city.

The best way to get around the site is by bicycle, though many opt for an air-conditioned minibus.

🅐 Malakor, a simple wooden restaurant on Chaikun Road, directly in front of Wat Ratchaburuna, serves a reasonable range of Thai and Western dishes.

• 53 miles (85 km) N of Bangkok
• Map T1
• Most temples: open 8am–5pm daily; adm B50 (some are free)
• Chao Sam Phraya National Museum: open 9am–4pm, Wed–Sun; adm B150
• Ayutthaya Historical Study Center: open 9am–4:30pm Mon–Fri and 9am–5pm Sat–Sun; adm B100

Top 10 Features

1. Wat Phra Mahathat
2. Chao Sam Phraya National Museum
3. Wat Ratchaburuna
4. Ayutthaya Historical Study Center
5. Wat Phra Si Sanphet
6. Wat Thammikarat
7. Wat Lokaya Sutharam
8. Wat Phra Ram
9. Wang Luang
10. Wihan Phra Mongkhon Bophit

Wat Phra Mahathat

During Ayutthaya's heyday, this was one of its most important temples with a large compound and a 151-ft (46-m) high laterite *prang* (tower), which has now collapsed. It remains one of the most evocative of all the city's sights, with smaller *prang* leaning at precarious angles and a serene Buddha's head encased by the roots of a banyan tree *(below)*.

Chao Sam Phraya National Museum

Most of Ayutthaya's precious artifacts, including gold Buddha images, were either taken by the invading Burmese or looters. A few remaining items are on show here *(above)*.

Wat Ratchaburuna

Next door to Wat Phra Mahathat and covering as large an area, this temple was built in 1424 by King Borommaracha II, and its main structure is a central, Khmer-style *prang*. In 1957, the crypt beneath the *prang* was opened by robbers, who made off with a horde of gold artifacts. The few items they did not take are now on display in the Chao Sam Phraya National Museum. The crypt can be reached by a steep staircase where there are beautiful Ayutthayan frescoes.

 Ayutthaya is named for the god Rama's kingdom in the Hindu epic Ramayana

4 Ayutthaya Historical Study Center

This study center *(below)* attempts to depict the city's history and trading relations, with models reproducing ships, houses, and other historical objects. It also houses a model of Wat Phra Si Sanphet, the former temple of which little now remains.

5 Wat Phra Si Sanphet

Once Ayutthaya's most glorious temple, all that is left of Wat Phra Si Sanphet *(above)* today, are three Sri Lankan-style *chedi* (stupas) and the ruins of former palaces. The *chedi* contain ashes of Ayutthayan kings and are the park's highlight.

6 Wat Thammikarat

One of the park's less visited, yet most atmospheric temples has the ruins of an octagonal *chedi*, a *wihan*, and a fearsome *singha (below)*.

7 Wat Lokaya Sutharam

The highlight of this temple is a huge, white-washed Reclining Buddha *(left)* exposed to the elements. Octagonal pillars around it once supported a wooden hall that sheltered the image.

A Short History of Ayutthaya

Ayutthaya was founded by King Ramathibodi I in 1350. Over the next four centuries, the kingdom came to dominate the region now known as Thailand, apart from the north, where the Kingdom of Lanna maintained its independence. Traders visited from Europe, returning home with tales of a highly organized and sophisticated society. The kingdom's end was as sudden as its inception, and its capital completely abandoned after being sacked by the Burmese in 1767.

10 Wihan Phra Mongkhon Bophit

This *wihan* (assembly hall) was built in the 1950s to shelter a massive bronze Buddha image that dates back to the 15th century and is over 40 ft (12 m) tall *(below)*.

8 Wat Phra Ram

Wat Phra Ram is one of Ayutthaya's oldest temples. Originally built in 1369, the main *prang*, decorated with *naga*, *garuda*, and Buddha images, was added in the 15th century.

9 Wang Luang

Built in the 15th century by King Boromatrailokanat, this royal palace had enough stable space for over 100 elephants. It was razed to the ground by the Burmese and today only the foundations are left.

In mid-December, Ayutthaya hosts a week-long festival to celebrate its UNESCO World Heritage status

Left **Wat Na Phra Mane** Center **Wat Yai Chai Mongkol** Right **Wat Phanan Choeng**

Sights In and Around Ayutthaya

1 Bang Pa-In
Included on many tours of Ayutthaya, this former royal summer retreat is an eclectic mix of Thai and Western architectural styles. The Aisawan Thipphaya-at pavilion that sits on a lake is its most photographed building.
⊗ *15 miles (24 km) S of Ayutthaya • Open 8:30am–4:30pm daily • Adm*

2 Lopburi
One of Thailand's oldest towns, Lopburi was an important center of Dvaravati culture from the 6th century onwards. Both King Narai *(see box)* and Rama IV *(see p34)* used it as a second capital, and Narai's palace is well worth a visit. ⊗ *44 miles (70 km) N of Ayutthaya*

3 Wat Na Phra Mane
This Ayutthayan temple was less badly damaged than most by the invading Burmese and is therefore one of the most interesting to explore. Inside the temple is a large *bot* (ordination hall), which displays some fine architectural features, and a small *wihan* (assembly hall) with a rare Dvaravati stone Buddha.
⊗ *N of Ayutthaya • Open 8am–5pm Mon–Fri, 8am–6pm Sat–Sun • Adm*

4 Wat Yai Chai Mongkol
The main features of this temple are a huge *chedi* (stupa) erected by King Naresuan, a host of saffron-robed, laterite Buddha images that surround it, and a large Reclining Buddha set in a corner of the temple grounds. ⊗ *1 mile (2 km) E of Ayutthaya • Open 8am–5pm daily • Adm*

5 Chantarakasem Palace Museum
Ayutthaya's oldest museum displays a throne platform that belonged to Rama IV, some beautiful ceramics and Buddha images, as well as cannons and muskets. ⊗ *NE corner of Ayutthaya • Open 8:30am–4:30pm Wed–Sun • Adm*

Chantarakasem Palace Museum

6 Wat Phu Khao Thong
Also known as the Golden Mount, this temple's main feature is a 263-ft (80-m) high *chedi*. It is possible to climb part of the way up the structure to get a panoramic view of the rice fields around.
⊗ *1 mile (2 km) W of Ayutthaya*

7 Wat Phanan Choeng
Particularly popular with Chinese worshippers because of a shrine to a Chinese princess, this temple dates back to the 14th century. Its centerpiece is a 62-ft (19-m) tall, seated bronze

image of Phra Chao Phanan Choeng. ◈ *S of Ayutthaya • Open 8am–5pm daily • Adm*

Wat Puthaisawan
Located across the river from central Ayutthaya, the temple has a restored 14th- century *prang* (tower) which is surrounded by cloisters packed with Buddha images. ◈ *S of Ayutthaya*

Wat Chai Wattanaram
Built in the 17th century and restored in the late 20th century, Wat Chai Wattanaram is modeled on Angkor Wat, with a central *prang* surrounded by eight smaller ones. ◈ *W of Ayutthaya*

Wat Chai Wattanaram

St. Joseph's Cathedral
A cathedral was built here in the 17th century to accommodate the needs of foreign merchants, who were not permitted to enter the city center except by invitation. It was renovated in the 19th century and is still functional. ◈ *W of Ayutthaya*

Top 10 Kings of Ayutthaya
1. Ramathibodi (r.1351–69)
2. Borommaracha I (r.1370–88)
3. Borommaracha II (r.1424–48)
4. Borommatrailokanat (r.1448–88)
5. Ramathibodi II (r.1491–1529)
6. Naresuan (r.1590–1605)
7. Prasat Thong (r.1629–56)
8. Narai (r.1656–88)
9. Phra Phetracha (r.1688–1703)
10. Phumintharacha (r.1758–67)

King Narai the Great (r.1656–88)

Like most kings of Ayutthaya, Narai was a usurper, having deposed his older brother to take the throne. He is best remembered for his warming of diplomatic relations with Western countries, his sending of missions to European courts, and his selection of a foreigner, Constantine Phaulkon, as his principal advisor. It was from reports by European merchants of this era that Ayutthaya became known in the west for its richness and splendor. Phaulkon encouraged Narai to balance Dutch interests in the kingdom by inviting a French delegation to visit. However, many Siamese suspected, quite correctly as it turned out, that the French mission's main objective was to convert the king to Christianity, and on Narai's death foreigners were banished from Ayutthaya.

Statue of King Naresuan

Complex of Wat Phra Si Rattana Mahathat, Lopburi

Left **Railroad Station** Right **Rama IV, King of Siam, with Queen Ramphuy**

Moments in History

1767: Ayutthaya Overrun by the Burmese

After 400 years of being one of Asia's most powerful empires, the Kingdom of Ayutthaya *(see pp28–31)* was finally overrun by Burmese troops in 1767. Though the Burmese were expelled within a year, Ayutthaya was deemed unsafe as a capital and General Taksin chose Thonburi as the new capital of Siam (now Thailand).

1782: Bangkok Founded

Just 15 years later, a rebellion against Taksin's autocratic rule led to his demise. He was succeeded by General Chao Phraya Chakri who established the Chakri Dynasty and acquired the official title of Rama I. On assuming the throne, his first action was to move the capital east across the river to Bangkok.

1851: Rama IV Crowned

After living 27 years as a monk, King Mongkut acceded to the throne and became Rama IV of the Chakri Dynasty. He is regarded by Thais as the man who began to modernize Siam, particularly through treaties that opened the country to trade with the West.

1868: Rama V Crowned

Chulalongkorn, son of Rama IV, succeeded his father as Rama V of the Chakri Dynasty when he was only 15 years old. He ruled for over 40 years and is credited with keeping Siam free from the clutches of colonial powers such as England and France, which were carving up Southeast Asia at the time.

Rama V, King of Siam (r.1868–1910)

1893: First Railroad Line

Rama V carried on his father's programme of modernization of the country, and in 1893 the country's first railroad line opened, stretching just 14 miles (22 km) to Pak Nam, where the Chao Phraya River flows into the Gulf of Thailand. The line was later extended to the south, north, and northeast of the country.

1932: Constitutional Monarchy

The absolute power of the Siamese monarchy was ended by a bloodless coup in 1932 that brought the military to power. Though the monarchy continued to be respected, the stage was set for a string of coups and counter coups that dominated the politics of Thailand for the rest of the century.

Preceding pages **Ayutthaya, the ancient capital of present-day Thailand**

Rama IX, the current King of Thailand

7 1946: Rama IX Ascends the Throne

After the death of his brother King Mahidol, who was shot in the head while in bed, King Bhumibol Adulyadej took the throne as Rama IX. He continues to rule as the world's longest-reigning monarch.

8 1992: Military Government Ousted

Thais demonstrated publicly their displeasure following a military coup in 1992. After the army gunned down many citizens on the streets of Bangkok, Rama IX intervened, resulting in the self-proclaimed Prime Minister, General Suchinda Kraprayoon, making a hasty exit and democracy being restored.

9 2006: Thaksin Ousted

Thailand's self-styled "CEO leader" Thaksin Shinawatra swept to power in 2001 as head of the Thai Rak Thai party, inspiring people with his business acumen. However, he was ousted for corruption in yet another military coup in September 2006.

10 2011: Thailand's First Female Prime Minister

Thaksin Shinawatra's sister Yingluck was elected Thailand's first female Prime Minister, and the youngest in over 60 years, in a landslide victory in 2011. One of the main goals of her Pheu Thai party is to return Thaksin from exile.

Top 10 Famous Thais

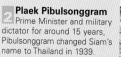

1 Chang and Eng Bunker
Born in Bangkok, the original Siamese Twins (1811–74) settled in the USA, married and fathered 22 children before dying within hours of each other.

2 Plaek Pibulsonggram
Prime Minister and military dictator for around 15 years, Pibulsonggram changed Siam's name to Thailand in 1939.

3 Kukrit Pramoj
Thailand's 13th prime minister (1975–6) was honored in 1985 as National Artist for his literary works.

4 Prem Tinsulanonda
The country's prime minister from 1980–88 and one of the closest advisors to King Rama IX.

5 Anand Panyarachun
Serving twice as prime minister in the early 1990s, he made long-overdue reforms to the Thai constitution in 1996.

6 Khaosai Galaxy
The "Thai Tyson", Khaosai was WBA Super Flyweight champion from 1984 to 1992, defending his title 19 times.

7 Porntip Nakhirunkanok
Crowned Miss Universe in 1988, she won this ultimate accolade for a country famed for its beautiful women.

8 Thongchai McIntyre
Known as "Bird," Thailand's biggest pop idol has also acted in movies and on TV.

9 Paradorn Srichaphan
Thailand's most successful tennis player appeared on the cover of *Time* and is known for his polite court manners.

10 Aum Patcharapa
This film and soap-opera star is Thailand's most famous actress and model.

Bangkok's Top 10

Thailand was officially known as Siam until 1939 and again between 1945 and 1949

35

Left **Suan Pakkad** Center **Jamjuree Gallery** Right **National Gallery**

🔟 Museums and Art Galleries

National Museum
An accurate overview of the evolution of Thai culture is represented in the National Museum *(see pp12–13)* through dioramas in the first hall, along with exquisite Sukhothai, Ayutthaya, Rattanakosin, and Lanna artifacts in other galleries. Don't miss the Ramkhamhaeng inscription, the Royal Funeral Chariots Gallery, and the Buddhaisawan Chapel.

Interior of the Buddhaisawan Chapel

National Gallery
Both traditional (starting from around the 17th century) and contemporary Thai art are featured at this gallery *(see p66)*. There are also many temporary exhibitions. Temple banners are displayed in the section upstairs. An art market is organized in the courtyard each weekend.

Royal Barge Museum
Housed in a dry-dock warehouse, this museum features eight gleaming barges, each nearly 165 ft (50 m) long, that are used only for special royal events. The biggest and most important barge, *Suphannahongse*, carries the king himself *(see p89)*.

Siriraj Medical Museums
This anomalous collection of skulls, pickled body parts, and murder weapons inside the Siriraj Hospital *(see p89)* is intended to educate rather than shock. Not for the squeamish, its most famous exhibit is the preserved corpse of Si Quey, a serial killer.

Suan Pakkad
A compound of traditional Thai houses, Suan Pakkad *(see p80)* is an excellent example of Thai architecture. The houses contain antique paintings, carvings, and a stunning display of masks used in *khon* (masked theater).

Thavibu Gallery
One of Bangkok's most impressive private galleries, Thavibu gets its name from the initial letters of Thailand, Vietnam, and Burma, the sources of most of its art. It promotes young artists who have a strong message. As well as the permanent collection, there are rotating exhibitions. ⬧ *Suite 433, Silom Galeria, 919/1 Silom Road • Map N6 • (02) 266 5454 • Open 11am–7pm Tue–Sat, noon–6pm Sun • www.thavibu.com*

H Gallery
Situated in a lovely colonial building on the backstreets of Silom Road, H Gallery mainly exhibits abstract works by contemporary Asian artists in a variety of media. Some works are quite innovative, such as the

rattan and wire sculptures by Cambodian artist Sopheap Pich. ◈ 201 Sathorn Soi 12 • Map N6 • (085) 021 5508 • Open 10am–6pm Wed–Mon • www.hgallerybkk.com

The Art Center, Chulalongkorn University

The Art Center

One of two galleries located on the campus grounds near Siam Square at Bangkok's prestigious Chulalongkorn University, The Art Center features work by professors from the university as well as by established Thai and international artists. The gallery is known for its experimental approach and interactive installations. ◈ Center of Academic Resources Building, Seventh Floor, Chulalongkorn University, Phaya Thai Road • Map P3 • (02) 218 2965 • Open 9am–7pm Mon–Fri, 9am–4pm Sat • www.car.chula.ac.th/art

Jamjuree Gallery

The second gallery at Chulalongkorn University is a two-story venue that showcases emerging artists, including students of the university's Faculty of Fine and Applied Arts, as well as established Thai artists and occasionally foreign artists. The gallery is an easy walk from Siam Square shopping district. ◈ Jamjuree Building 8, Chulalongkorn University, Phaya Thai Road • Map P3 • (02) 218 3708–9 • Open 10am–7pm Mon–Fri, noon–6pm Sat–Sun

The Queen's Gallery

Established in 2003 at the request of Queen Sirikit, this gallery is set in a five-story building and occupies a massive 39,825 sq ft (3,700 sq m) of exhibition space. The Queen wanted to showcase leading examples of Thai visual art. The gallery's shop stocks an interesting range of glossy art books and T-shirts featuring contemporary art. ◈ 101 Ratchadamnoen Klang • Map D3 • (02) 281 5360–1 • Open 10am–7pm Thu–Tue • Adm • www.queengallery.org

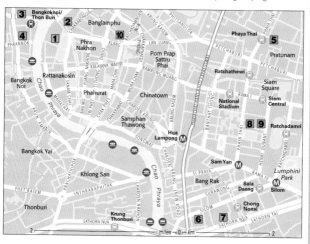

Left **Chatuchak Weekend Market** Right **Sampeng Lane Market**

🔟 Markets and Shopping

1 Chatuchak Weekend Market

Every weekend, the mother of all Thai markets, Chatuchak, throngs with young people looking for fashion accessories, middle-aged Thais wanting to decorate their homes, and foreigners looking for souvenirs of their stay in Thailand *(see pp22–3)*.

2 Pratunam Market

Cluttering the sidewalk and spilling over into several small lanes, this bustling market is a source of cheap clothing. Shops are packed with seamstresses bent over sewing machines. The market is also a good place to buy discount toiletries, suitcases and bags, mobile phone accessories, electronic equipment, and cheap souvenirs. 🖎 *Ratchaprarop Road • Map Q1 • Open 9am–midnight daily*

3 Phahurat Market

You would be forgiven for thinking you are in India when walking along the narrow streets of Phahurat Market. Shop after shop sells bolts of cloth, and there are plenty of cut-price travel agents and cheap cafés *(see p73)*.

4 Sampeng Lane Market

The market held on this narrow street is lined with shops selling household goods, fashion accessories, shoes, and clothing. Phahurat Road leads straight into Sampeng Lane, and walking from one to the other feels like hopping from India to China *(see p75)*.

5 Siam Paragon

This mall is one of the favorite hangouts of Bangkok's more fussy shoppers. With six floors full of designer clothes, cosmetics, nail studios, hairdressers, restaurants, cinemas, and book and music shops, Siam Paragon shopping mall has something for everyone. The superb aquarium, Siam Ocean World *(see p47)*, is located in the basement. 🖎 *Rama I Road, Siam Square • Map P2 • (02) 690 1000 • Open 10am–10pm daily • www.siamparagon.co.th*

Siam Paragon

6 Mahboonkrong

While most of Bangkok's shopping malls have a clinical, international feel to them, Mahboonkrong is totally Thai. Also known as MBK, this shopping mall sprawls across six floors. It is packed with small stalls selling souvenirs and cheap clothes that include copies of designer brands. There are also bigger retail outlets selling jewelry as well as a branch of the Tokyu Department Store. 🖎 *Phaya Thai Road • Map P3 • Open 10am–10pm daily • www.mbk-center.co.th*

Gaysorn Plaza

This shopping mall pitches itself at the upper classes with designer boutiques, beauty salons, exclusive craft outlets, and pricey restaurants. The second floor features "Urban Chic Street," where several Thai fashion designers have a display. Gaysorn Lifestyle Consultants proactively advise shoppers. ⦿ *Ploenchit Road • Map Q2 • (02) 656 1149 • Open 10am–8pm daily • www.gaysorn.com*

Pantip Plaza

Pantip Plaza

This is an IT mecca, selling all the latest computer programs and DVD movies, as well as digital cameras and other electronic equipment. Although it is crammed with new and used hardware and software, the mall is rife with counterfeit products. Despite regular police raids, vendors dealing in pirated goods seem to keep in business thanks to their customers' huge appetite for such stuff. ⦿ *New Phetburi Road • Map Q2 • (02) 250 1555 • Open 10am–10pm daily • www.pantipplaza.com*

River City

The River City Shopping Complex is an upmarket shopping center selling antiques, crafts, and Thai silk, and is operated by Mandarin Oriental and the Italthai Group. Located on the banks of the Chao Phraya, it has several restaurants with river views where customers can relax after browsing the art and antique shops on the third and fourth floors. ⦿ *Yotha Road, off Charoen Krung Road • Map M4 • (02) 237 0077 • Open 10am–10pm daily • www.rivercity.co.th*

Narai Phand

If it is gifts for family and friends that you are looking for, head along to this shop that specializes in Thai handicrafts. The choice available ranges from Thai dolls to *khon* theatrical masks and brass statues, from lacquerware and woodcarvings to silk clothing and silverware. However, unlike in almost all markets around Thailand, there is no bargaining here. ⦿ *973 Ploenchit Road • Map Q2 • (02) 656 0398 • Open 10am–8pm daily • www.naraiphand.com*

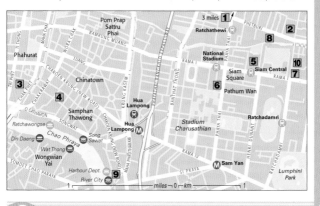

Left **Blue Elephant** Center **Cabbages & Condoms** Right **Views from Sirocco**

🔟 Restaurants

1 Le Normandie

One of Bangkok's best restaurants, Le Normandie serves top-notch French food and has a relaxing ambience, lavish decor, and impeccable service. Specialties include goose liver ravioli with truffle cream sauce, Brittany half lobster, and roast lamb in tomato crust. They also have over 200 French wines *(see p85)*.

Le Normandie

2 Maha Naga

Tucked away just a few strides from the busy Sukhumvit Road, both the garden and indoor seating at this beautifully laid-out restaurant offer a tranquil haven. The food is mostly Thai fusion, though many traditional Thai dishes are also on the menu, and service is very attentive *(see p93)*.

3 Sirocco

Situated on the rooftop of a skyscraper, Sirocco has stunning, panoramic views of the city and the food does not disappoint. Specialties include Mediterranean shellfish salad, grilled Maine lobster, and charbroiled marinated rack of lamb. It has an excellent range of wines, though some

cost over B100,000 per bottle. Sirocco also holds regular live jazz performances *(see p85)*.

4 Breeze

Breeze takes the notion of exclusivity a step further with its focus on Asian seafood. The fabulous views, superb service, and delicious cuisine make dining here a memorable experience, though it comes at a price, with some dishes costing well over B3,000 *(see p85)*.

5 Blue Elephant

With successful outlets around the world, this restaurant serves royal Thai cuisine. The menu features delights such as Pearls of Blue Elephant, a variety of starters on one plate, and main dishes such as larb salmon and lemongrass steak *(see p93)*.

6 Himali Cha Cha

Decorated in old-world Indian style, this restaurant serves up some excellent Indian food, including delicious *dal*, spicy prawn *dopiaza*, and kebabs grilled in a tangy sauce. For those who like their food not too spicy, the *biryani* are a good choice. If you have room, finish with a *kulfi*, a nutty Indian ice cream *(see p85)*.

7 Baan Khanitha

Frequently winning awards for its food, Baan Khanitha serves Thai cuisine in a traditional setting. Popular here are the national dish *tom yam kung*, prawns in sour

Most top-end restaurants accept credit cards

and spicy soup, and *yam som o*, a spicy pomelo salad with chicken and prawn *(see p93)*.

Le Lys
More like a home than a restaurant, this place is very welcoming and even has a petanque lawn for anyone who fancies a game. The food is reliably good, with dishes including fresh lemongrass salad, grilled sea bass with Thai herbs, and grilled duck red curry. It has a good selection of wines *(see p93)*.

Le Lys

Cabbages & Condoms
This restaurant with an unusual name is run by the Population and Community Development Association of Thailand – thus the focus on family planning – and has the curious motto: "Our food is guaranteed not to cause pregnancy." It serves some tasty dishes such as spicy catfish salad and prawns steamed in coconut *(see p93)*.

Basil
Located in the Sheraton Grande Sukhumvit *(see p113)*, this wonderfully inventive restaurant offers Thai cuisine at its most sophisticated. With more than 100 dishes on the menu there is something for all palates. Stir-fried lobster with cashew nuts and chilli is just one of the many superb main course dishes *(see p93)*.

Top 10 Culinary Highlights

1 Tom Yam Kung
Thailand's signature dish – a hot and spicy soup with chilies, lemongrass, and galangal – is typically served with prawns or seafood.

2 Phat Thai
Literally "Thai fry," this delicious noodle dish with beansprouts, peanuts, and eggs is a great lunchtime filler.

3 Kaeng Phanaeng
This thick curry made with coconut cream is usually served with pork or chicken.

4 Nam Prik Num
This delicious, gooey dip made of pounded chilies and eggplant seems to typify Thai cuisine with its spicy taste and creamy texture.

5 Sticky Rice
Thais from the north and northeast press a ball of sticky rice into their dips and sauces.

6 Som Tam
Unripe (green) papaya is shredded finely and mixed with dried shrimp, lemon juice, tomatoes, peanuts, fish sauce, and chilies to make this salad.

7 Phat Pak Bung
Morning glory, one of Thailand's tastiest greens, is fried with garlic in oyster sauce for this crunchy, nutritious dish.

8 Mango with Sticky Rice
A delicious dessert of ripe mango with sticky rice and a coconut milk sauce.

9 Coconut Custard
This is a sweet filling of coconut milk, eggs, and sugar.

10 Fruit Juices and Shakes
Most Thai fruits can be served as thirst-quenching juices or shakes with yoghurt.

Left **Brown Sugar: The Jazz Boutique** Center **Q Bar** Right **Witch's Tavern**

🔟 Bars and Clubs

1 Adhere the 13th
This tiny hole-in-the-wall bar near Khao San Road has a welcoming atmosphere. The house band plays mostly blues and jazz from around 10pm, with special weekend events proving to be the crowd-pullers. Drinks are reasonably priced. ✪ *13 Samsen Road • Map C2 • Open 6pm–midnight daily*

Saxophone, Bangkok

2 Saxophone
The music played here is impressive with good live jazz on weeknights, rock and blues at the weekend, and occasional reggae jam sessions on a Sunday. Prices are moderate. ✪ *3/8 Victory Monument, Phaya Thai Road • Map T5 • (02) 246 5472 • Open 6pm–2am daily • www.saxophonepub.com*

3 Brown Sugar: The Jazz Boutique
The city's premier jazz venue is a Bangkok institution. A restaurant and coffee house by day, at night it is a bar featuring an acoustic set followed by the resident jazz band. ✪ *469 Wanchad Junction, Phra Sumen Road • Map D3 • (02) 282 0396 • Open 11am–1am Sun–Thu, 11am–2am Fri–Sat• www.brownsugarbangkok.com*

4 Bed Supperclub
Resembling a space station, this ultra-modern club with a swanky restaurant has Bangkok's most popular dance floor. ✪ *26 Sukhumvit Soi 11 • Map T6 • (02) 651 3537 • Open 8pm–2am daily • www.bedsupperclub.com*

5 Q Bar
A favorite among both locals and visitors, Q Bar often hosts weekend parties with international DJs. Music varies from hip-hop to house, acid jazz to drum and bass. ✪ *34 Sukhumvit Soi 11 • Map T6 • (02) 252 3274 • Open 8pm–2am daily • www.qbarbangkok.com*

6 Bamboo Bar
With its relaxed atmosphere, this is a great spot to unwind and listen to smooth jazz. ✪ *Oriental Hotel, 48 Oriental Avenue • Map M5 • (02) 236 0400 • Open 11am–12:45am Fri & Sat,11am–11:45pm Sun–Thu*

Hard Rock Café

7 Hard Rock Café
The Bangkok branch of this international chain features a guitar-shaped bar that stocks a wide range of cocktails and

beers. Rock bands usually get the audience dancing from around 10pm. There is a decent menu and the bar's happy hours are from 5pm to 8pm.

S 424/3–6 Soi 11, Siam Square • Map P3 • (02) 658 4090 • Open 11:30am–1am daily • www.hardrock.com/bangkok

Lucifer, Bangkok

Lucifer
This popular dance club located on Bangkok's notorious Patpong is decorated with stalactites, mosaics, and red-eyed demon masks that gaze down on the dance floor. Staff serve drinks wearing orange uniforms with devil's horns.
S 76/1–3 Patpong 1 • Map P5 • (02) 234 6902 • Open 9:30pm–2am daily

RCA
Royal City Avenue is a popular entertainment zone lined with trendy dance clubs, such as Route 66 and 808, as well as restaurants and noodle stands. Young city workers and students regard it as party central. S Rama IX Road, Soi 8 • Map U5 • Open till 2am daily

Witch's Tavern
Live bands play every night at this popular venue, usually beginning with some gentle folk or jazz music, and gradually picking up the pace as the night wears on. The house band plays mostly covers of favorite rock ballads. S 306/1 Sukhumvit Soi 55 • Map T6• (02) 391 9791 • Open 11am–1am daily • www.witch-tavern.com

Top 10 Gay Bars and Clubs

1 The Balcony
At the heart of Bangkok's gay scene, the Balcony bar offers cheap food and evening happy hours. S Silom Soi 4 • Map P5

2 Coffee Society
Occupying four floors, this café is also a cruising spot, a chill-out lounge, and art gallery. S Silom Road (between Soi 2 and Soi 4) • Map P5

3 Disco Disco
This bar/disco is a good place to see and be seen. S Silom Soi 2 • Map P5

4 DJ Station
A popular gay disco which is packed almost every night. S Silom Soi 2 • Map P5

5 The Expresso
This is a good place to chill out and watch the street action. S Silom Soi 2 • Map P5

6 X Boom
The party really gets going here after midnight. S Surawong Road • Map P4

7 G.O.D.
Guys on Display, or G.O.D., is an aptly-named gay bar that has a big dance area. S Silom Road (between Soi 2 and Soi 4) • Map P5

8 Telephone Pub
This pub is named after the phones that once offered intimate table-to-table contact. S 114/11–13 Silom Soi 4 • Map P5

9 Sphinx
The good range of food served at this bar appeals to a classy crowd. S 104 Silom Soi 4 • Map P5

10 Vega Café
For women, this venue gets packed at weekends. S Sukhumvit Soi 39 • Map T6

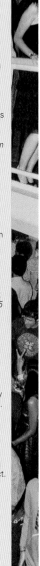

Left **A rehearsal at the National Theatre** Center **Siam Niramit** Right **Cabaret, Playhouse Theater**

Entertainment Venues

Aksra Theatre
1 Located in the Pullman King Power hotel complex downtown, the Aksra Theatre's puppet shows feature stunning set designs and elaborate Thai puppets costumed in traditional dress. Performances include the Hindu epic *Ramakien*, Thai folk dances, and Japanese songs. ⊗ *8/1 Rangnam Road, Thanon-Phayathai, Ratchathewi • Map T5 • (02) 677 8888 • Show 7:30pm Mon–Wed • Adm • www.aksratheatre.com*

Puppeteers at the Aksra Theatre

Siam Niramit
2 This cultural extravaganza designed for tourists presents an idealized vision of ancient Siam using hi-tech special effects, lavish costumes, and a cast of hundreds. ⊗ *Ratchada Theater, 19 Tiam Ruammit Road • Map T5 • (02) 649 9222 • Show 8pm daily • Adm • www.siamniramit.com*

National Theatre
3 Impressive productions of Thai classical drama and *khon* (masked theater) with skilled actors and sumptuous costumes are staged at the National Theatre on the last Friday of every month. Modern Thai dramas and musical performances are also staged here. ⊗ *Rachini Road • Map B3 • (02) 224 1342 • Adm*

Playhouse Theater
4 Once housing the Calypso Cabaret (*see p45*), the Asia Hotel is now home to an equally extravagant theater and dance show. The Playhouse ladyboy cabaret features glamorous Thai dancers, elaborate stage sets, and well-known songs from musicals. ⊗ *Asia Hotel, 296 Phayathai Road • Map P2 • (02) 215 0571 • Show 8:15pm, 9:45pm daily • Adm • www.playhousethailand.com*

Silom Village
5 A show featuring various forms of Thai dance and martial arts demonstrations, accompanied by dinner, is staged at Silom Village. The standard of the performance and quality of the food make it a good choice for an evening's entertainment. ⊗ *Silom Road • Map N5 • (02) 234 4448 • Indoor show with set dinner 8:20–9:15pm daily • Adm*

Thailand Cultural Centre
6 Bangkok's main center for the performing arts, this state-run facility is home to the Bangkok Symphony Orchestra. It also hosts the annual International Festival of Dance and Music. International artists also perform here during world tours, so check for upcoming events. ⊗ *Ratchadaphisek Road • Map T5 • (02) 247 0028 • www.thaiculturalcenter.com*

Dinner theater offers a restaurant meal combined with a staged play

Sala Rim Naam

7 This dinner theater operated by the Oriental Hotel *(see p79)* is a custom-built facility offering a classy show of traditional Thai dance accompanied by a gourmet dinner. Prices are above average but the event is memorable.

Ⓢ *Oriental Hotel • (02) 437 3080*
• Lunch: noon–2pm daily; dinner theater: 7–10pm daily; show: 8:30–9:30pm daily
• www.mandarinoriental.com

Calypso Cabaret

Calypso Cabaret

8 Cabarets performed by transvestites are popular in Thailand. This show involves a cast of glamorous lookers in lavish costumes lip-synching to pop songs.
Ⓢ *Asiatique The Riverfront, 2194 Charoen Krung 72–76 Road • Map S6 • (02) 688 1415 • Show 8:15pm, 9:45pm daily • Adm*
• www.calypsocabaret.com

Ratchadamnoen Boxing Stadium

9 It is worth attending an evening of *muay Thai*, or Thai boxing *(see p54)*, at this stadium, not only for the excitement of watching the contestants punching and kicking each other around the ring, but also to see how worked up the Thai spectators get during the bouts. Add the strange dances performed by the boxers to the accompaniment of wailing instruments before each fight, and you have an evening of exotic, Oriental entertainment.
Ⓢ *1 Ratchadamnoen Nok Road • Map E2 • (02) 281 4205 • Bouts: 6:30–11pm Mon, Wed, Thu; 5–8pm and 8:30pm–midnight Sun • Adm*

Sala Chalermkrung Royal Theatre

10 Built in 1933 by Rama VII, this was Thailand's first theater to be built with the intention of screening "talking pictures." Today it is used for staging *khon* (masked theater) and for live performances by singers and musicians.
Ⓢ *Charoen Krung Road • Map C5*
• (02) 222 0434 • Khon: 8:30pm Fri & Sat
• www.salachalermkrung.com

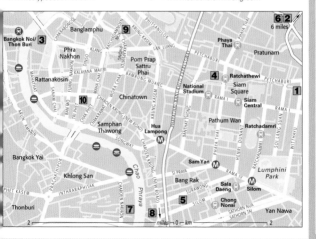

Left **Bangkok Dolls Museum** Right **Bangkok Planetarium**

Children's Attractions

Safari World
A favorite with kids, the attractions at Safari World include a jungle walk and cruise, safari terrace, marine park, and spy war zone as well as orangutan boxing, Hollywood cowboy stunts and dolphin, bird, and sea lion shows. *99 Panyaintra Road, Minburi • Map U4 • (02) 518 1000 • Open 9am–5pm daily • Adm • www.safariworld.com*

Children's Discovery Museum
A veritable heaven for curious kids, hands-on exhibits include a studio where children can make TV shows. They can also learn about life underground and watch a puppet show. *Queen Sirikit Park, Kamphaenphet Road • Map T5 • (02) 615 7333 • Closed for renovations; phone for latest information*

Children's Discovery Museum

Dusit Zoo
This zoo was initiated a century ago by Rama V *(see p34)*, who had been impressed by the zoos he saw in Europe and was aware of their power to educate.

Today, Dusit Zoo contains all the big mammals – lions, tigers, elephants, bears, and hippos – as well as lots of slithery reptiles and colorful birds. A kids' playground, elephant rides, pedalos on the lake, refreshment kiosks, and shady picnic areas add to the zoo's appeal. *77 Rama V Road • Map F1 • (02) 282 7111 • Open 8am–6pm daily • Adm • www.zoothailand.org*

Bangkok Dolls Museum
This museum was created by Tongkorn Chandavimol in the 1950s after a visit to Japan, which aroused her interest in the various types of dolls from different countries and periods of history. The dolls on display, from her own collection, are from all over the world. Dolls can be purchased for around B400–500. The museum is tricky to find, but well worth the effort. *85 Soi Mo Leng, Ratchaprarop Road • Map T5 • (02) 245 3008 • Open 8am–5pm Mon–Sat • Free • www.bangkokdolls.com*

Bangkok Planetarium
Aspects of the universe are projected onto a huge domed ceiling at this planetarium. There are also exhibits on space travel, astronomy through the ages, and the life of stars and the solar system, as well as a separate computer zone and an aquarium. Allow at least half a day to see everything of interest. *928 Sukhumvit Road • Map T6 • (02) 391 0544 • Open 8:30am–4:30pm Tue–Sun • Adm • www.sciplanet.org*

Siam Park
6 Located in the outskirts of the city, Siam Park is a water park, amusement park, and themed attraction rolled into one. The highlights of the water park are a speed slide, a super spiral, and a wave pool. The amusement park has a mini carousel, a swan boat, and adventure safari, while the theme park has a Jurassic adventure and a miniature train. 🅢 99 Seri Thai Road, Kanna Yaow • Map U5 • (02) 919 7200–5 • Open 10am–6pm daily • Adm • www.siamparkcity.com

Dream World

Dream World
7 This amusement park has four main areas: Dream World Plaza, Dream Garden, Fantasy Land, and Adventure Land. A sightseeing train runs around the Dream Garden, which has models of world-famous sights such as the Great Wall of China and the Taj Mahal. 🅢 62 Moo 1, Rangsit-Nakornnayok Road, Thanyaburi, Pathumthani • Map T2 • (02) 577 8666 • Open 10am–5pm Mon–Fri, 10am–7pm Sat & Sun • Adm

Lumphini Park
8 Named for the birthplace of the Buddha in Nepal, this is the only decent-sized park in the center of Bangkok. Though slightly crowded at times, it has a pleasant environment with lots of shady trees, picnic spots, and a large lake (see p80).

Siam Ocean World
9 One of the largest aquariums in Southeast Asia, the superb Siam Ocean World is divided into seven zones, which include Deep Reef, Living Ocean, and Rocky Shore. Attractions include glass-bottom boat rides and the chance to dive with sharks. There are also penguin and shark feeding sessions, plus a Magical Mermaid Show. 🅢 Basement, Siam Paragon, Rama I Road • Map P2 • (02) 687 2000 • Open 9am–10pm daily • Adm • www.siamoceanworld.co.th

Snake Farm
10 Founded as the Pasteur Institute in 1923, the Queen Saovabha Memorial Institute, better known as the Snake Farm, is now run by the Red Cross. Venom-milking sessions of cobras and pit vipers take place at 11am daily, with an extra session on weekdays at 2:30pm. Brave visitors can also get a souvenir photo with a snake curled around their neck (see p81).

Left **Chinese New Year parade** Right **Songkran festival**

🔟 Festivals

1 River of Kings
Celebrating the Chao Phraya River, this festival takes place at night for two weeks in late January/early February. Shows glorifying Thai heroes of the past through song, dance, drama, and animation can be viewed from a floating stadium or luxury river cruisers. ◈ *Chao Phraya River in front of Grand Palace • Map B4 • (02) 623 5500 extn. 1120–22 • Shows at 7pm and 9:15pm • Adm*

Traditional barges beside the Grand Palace

2 Chinese New Year
This week-long Thai-Chinese celebration in January or February has lion dances in the street, lots of loud firecrackers, and colorful activities in temples. Most Chinese businesses close down for the week. ◈ *Chinatown*

3 Makha Puja
This annual Buddhist festival, held at the full moon in February or March, celebrates the Buddha's first sermon to 1,250 disciples, starting the dissemination of the *dhamma*. Buddhists walk around *chedi* (stupas) offering lit candles, incense, and lotus. ◈ *Nationwide*

4 Songkran
Thai New Year, celebrated in mid-April, is the country's most chaotic and raucous festival. People throw water over each other as a symbolic form of cleansing to usher in the New Year, and even passers-by are not spared. Perhaps for its novelty value, this festival is particularly popular among foreign visitors. ◈ *Nationwide • www.tourismthailand. org/see-do/event-festival*

5 International Festival of Dance and Music
Since 1999, Bangkok's premier arts festival has been held at the Thailand Cultural Centre *(see p44)* in September and October each year. It features performers from around the world, along with Thailand's best. The focus of the festival is on opera, ballet, and classical music, though jazz and modern dance are represented as well.

6 Royal Ploughing Ceremony
One of Bangkok's most ancient ceremonies, this annual event, which takes place in early May, is designed to give an auspicious start to the new planting season. Sacred white oxen are used to plough a ritual field in Sanam Luang *(see p63)* near the Grand Palace *(see pp8–9)*, which is then sown with rice seeds blessed by the king, after which farmers rush to collect the blessed seeds to plant in their own fields.

Dhamma, *a Buddhist concept, is the enlightened path that leads to personal liberation*

7 Loy Krathong

This festival, usually held in November, offers homage to the goddess of the waters for providing a successful harvest. Beautiful *krathong* (small decorated floats) are released onto the river at night amid fireworks. ◈ *Nationwide*

Festival of Loy Krathong

8 Wat Saket Fair

Temple fairs in Thailand are like village fêtes in the West, and this one at Wat Saket and the Golden Mount *(see p64)*, held just before or after Loy Krathong, is a good example. It has a great atmosphere, with music and theater on makeshift stages and kids having fun.

9 Bangkok International Film Festival

Held every year, usually in the autumn, this film festival showcases over 100 films from countries all around the world, with a particular emphasis on emerging film-makers throughout Asia. ◈ *www.worldfilmbkk.com*

10 King's Birthday

On December 5, a national holiday and also Fathers' Day, visitors have an opportunity to witness the reverence the Thai people feel for their monarch. Streets in the city center are decorated, fireworks light up the Grand Palace *(see pp8–9)*, and musicians and singers perform at Sanam Luang *(see p63)*.

Top 10 Up-Country Festivals

1 Chiang Mai Flower Festival
A parade of marching bands precedes floats bedecked with flowers. ◈ *First weekend, Feb*

2 ASEAN Barred Ground Dove Festival
This dove-singing contest attracts competitors to Yala from all over Southeast Asia. ◈ *First week, Mar*

3 Pattaya Music Festival
Hip-hop, rock, jazz, and easy-listening tunes are performed here by Thai musicians and international acts. ◈ *Mar*

4 Poy Sang Long
A Shan festival held in Chiang Mai and Mae Hong Son in which ordaining novices are paraded round the streets. ◈ *First weekend, Apr*

5 Rocket Festival
In the northeast, especially in Yasothon, home-made rockets are fired to trigger the start of the monsoons. ◈ *May*

6 Hua Hin Jazz Festival
This beach festival attracts some big names. ◈ *Jun*

7 Phi Ta Khon
Locals in Dan Sai dress as spirits for this wild and colorful event. ◈ *Jun/Jul*

8 Phuket Vegetarian Festival
Bizarre acts of self-mortification draw in the crowds for nine days. ◈ *Oct*

9 Lanna Boat Races
Held at the end of the Buddhist Lent with the most exciting races held in Nan Province. ◈ *Oct/Nov*

10 Elephant Round-Up
Surin, in the northeast, is the venue for this pachyderm extravaganza featuring games and parades. ◈ *Nov*

Jomtien Beach, Pattaya

Beaches Near Bangkok

Hua Hin
Thailand's oldest beach resort was popularized by the royal family when they had a summer palace built here in 1926. Though the 3-mile (5-km) beach is fine for a stroll or a pony ride, shade is limited, and the shallow bay can frustrate swimmers. Vestiges of the past remain in the train station and the squid piers along the front. There are some good seafood restaurants in the area. ◈ 118 miles (190 km) SW of Bangkok • Map S3

Cha Am
Though nearer to Bangkok than Hua Hin, Cha Am is not as popular. A quieter beach alternative, it is frequented by Thai families and students, and is now also starting to attract more foreign visitors to its string of high-rise hotels along the front. Casuarina trees provide good shade and swimming is possible, though the water is sometimes murky. ◈ 100 miles (161 km) SW of Bangkok • Map S3

Koh Si Chang
Rarely visited by foreigners, this small, rocky island is located 5 miles (8 km) off the east Gulf coast. It has a selection of everything – secluded beaches with clear waters, a hilly interior ripe for exploring, the remains of Rama V's palace, and some reasonable accommodations. The most popular beach is Tham Phang Beach. ◈ 62 miles (99 km) SE of Bangkok • Map U3

Pattaya Beach
The nearest mainland beach to Bangkok, Pattaya is very easy to get to from Suvarnabhumi, the international airport. While the town's reputation rests more on its nightlife than its golden sands, it boasts a reasonable stretch of beach and offers various watersports. Seafood and cold drinks hawkers stroll the shores. ◈ 103 miles (165 km) SE of Bangkok • Map U3

Pattaya Beach

Naklua Beach (Pattaya)
Located just north of Pattaya City, Naklua Beach is the quietest of Pattaya's three beaches, and still retains its fishing village charm despite the encroaching condominiums. There are only a couple of big hotels here, but the village has several seafood restaurants. Overlooking the beach is the unusual Sanctuary of Truth, a massive wooden building covered with intricate carvings. ◈ 103 miles (165 km) SE of Bangkok • Map U3

Jomtien Beach (Pattaya)
The southernmost beach in Pattaya, Jomtien, is a bit quieter than the town's main beach but

Preceding pages **Royal barges on the Chao Phraya River**

is backed by plenty of high-rise hotels, whose occupants sun themselves on this 9-mile (14-km) strip of sand. The beach has a reputation as Thailand's top windsurfing spot. Waterskiing, parasailing, and scuba diving are also on offer and there are several golf courses nearby. ⊗ *103 miles (165 km) SE of Bangkok • Map U3*

Mermaid statues at Hat Sai Kaeo

Hat Sai Kaeo (Koh Samed)
An offshore island within easy reach of Bangkok, Koh Samed has inviting beaches, with superb clear water and soft sand. Hat Sai Kaeo, or Diamond Beach, is the longest and most-easily accessible beach on the island. It is also the busiest, with a string of resorts drawing in tourists. It is wise to avoid week-ends when there is a shortage of accommodations. ⊗ *125 miles (200 km) SE of Bangkok • Map U3*

Ao Wong Deuan (Koh Samed)
Located half-way down the east coast of Koh Samed, Ao Wong Deuan, or Moon Bay, is the island's second-most popular beach. Several ferries a day head directly to this bay from Ban Phe (Rayong Province). There are some attractive accommo-dation options and the place is a bit

more peaceful than Hat Sai Kaeo, except in the center where there is a clutch of bars. ⊗ *125 miles (200 km) SE of Bangkok • Map U3*

Ao Thian (Koh Samed)
The candles that used to flicker in the bungalows before electricity arrived here lend the beach its name – Ao Thian, or Candlelight Bay. It now offers air-conditioned accommodations built along a hillside, but fortunately the laid-back image conjured up by its name still prevails. The narrow bay is interspersed with huge, smooth boulders that give it a very distinctive character. ⊗ *125 miles (200 km) SE of Bangkok • Map U3*

Ao Prao (Koh Samed)
The only beach on Koh Samed's west coast, Ao Prao, or Paradise Bay, has been com-mandeered by expensive resorts. The island is so narrow it is possible to stay on the east coast and walk across to the west coast to watch the sunset. There is a dive center here, as well as kayak and boat tours on offer. ⊗ *125 miles (200 km) SE of Bangkok • Map U3*

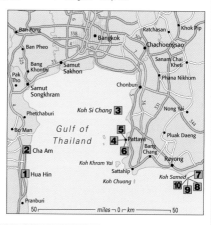

Left **Midday golf** Right **A *takraw* match in progress**

Sport and Leisure

Thai Boxing
Muay Thai (Thai boxing) has enjoyed an explosion of popularity of late, particularly among young Westerners, and many spend their holidays in Thailand practising this demanding sport in camps. For less active visitors to the kingdom, attending an evening of bouts at the Ratchadamnoen Boxing Stadium *(see p45)* is as much a cultural as a sporting experience.

Thai boxing

Horse Racing
There are a couple of race courses in Bangkok – the Royal Turf Club (RTC) in Dusit and the Royal Bangkok Sports Club (RBSC). Races are held fortnightly at each course, on alternate Sundays at RBSC *(see p82)* and RTC. The minimum bet is B50. The Saphan Taksin line of the Skytrain provides a bird's-eye view of the RBSC. ◈ *RTC: Phitsanulok Road • Map F2 • (02) 280 0020–9 • Adm*

Takraw
Best described as volleyball played with the feet, Takraw is visually exciting, with the players performing acrobatic feats to kick the ball over the net. Games are played in Sanam Luang *(see p63)*, public parks, or any small open space in Bangkok.

Golf
This game is very popular among visitors to Bangkok for a variety of reasons – courses are generally of a high international standard, with scenic landscaping, very competitive equipment rental and green fees, and attentive and friendly service. There are several golf courses within easy reach of Bangkok.

Bowling
A great way of spending a fun afternoon or evening with friends is to go bowling. It offers a sporting challenge without too much exertion. Most of Bangkok's shopping malls have a bowling alley on the top floor, some of which are equipped with karaoke facilities and disco lighting.

Tennis
Following the success of Thai tennis hero Paradorn Srichaphan *(see p35)*, tennis has become very popular among Thais. It is advisable to play early in the morning or late in the afternoon to avoid the searing heat. Major hotels have private tennis courts; public courts are at the National Stadium and in Lumphini Park *(see p80)*. ◈ *National Stadium: 154 Rama I Rd • Map N2 • (02) 214 0120*

7 Ice Skating
The last thing a visitor can imagine on a tropical holiday are ice rinks, but there are a few on the outskirts of Bangkok. Qualified coaches are on hand to teach beginners how to glide across the ice. ◎ *Sub Zero: Esplanade, Ratchadaphisek Road • Map T5 • (02) 354 2134 • Open 11am–midnight daily • Adm*

8 Swimming
To cool off, plunge into a pool at a top-end or mid-range hotel. There are public pools at the National Stadium and the sports center at the Chuklalongkorn University *(see p82)*.

9 Martial Arts
It is possible to study and practise all kinds of martial arts in Bangkok, from Thai boxing to *tae kwan do*, judo, or karate, though probably the most popular is *t'ai chi*. To join the city's inhabitants for an impromptu session of *t'ai chi* or aerobics, head along to Lumphini Park *(see p80)* at dawn or dusk.

A morning session of *t'ai chi*

10 Snooker
Since James Wattana joined the world rankings, snooker has become hugely popular in Thailand. There are now thousands of clubs across the country, with hundreds of them in Bangkok. Tables are usually in excellent condition, cues are on hand for borrowing, and hourly rates are very reasonable.

Top 10 Thai Sporting Events

1 International Kite Festival
Both individual and team events are held and unusual kites are on show. ◎ *Hua Hin • Mar*

2 Chiang Mai Cricket Sixes
A fun event with big names turning up occasionally. ◎ *Apr*

3 Koh Samui Regatta
One of the highlights of the Asian sailing circuit. ◎ *May/Jun*

4 Phuket Marathon
This marathon attracts thousands of entries each year. ◎ *Jun*

5 International Mountain Bike Competition
Riders traverse the hills around the Bhumibol Dam. ◎ *Tak • Aug*

6 Thailand Tennis Open
A very popular and prestigious tennis tournament. ◎ *Bangkok • Sep*

7 King's Cup Elephant Polo Tournament
Unusual event in which elephants and *mahouts* (elephant keeper and driver) chase a ball around a field. ◎ *Golden Triangle • Sep*

8 Chonburi Buffalo Races
Farmers ride their buffaloes bareback in this annual pageant. ◎ *Oct*

9 Laguna Phuket Triathlon
A gruelling challenge for athletes in a sport that tests their swimming, cycling, and running skills. ◎ *Dec*

10 King's Cup Regatta
Since its inception in 1987, this has become Asia's premier international sailing event, with prizes for many classes of yacht. ◎ *Phuket • Dec*

Left **Banyan Tree Spa, Banyan Tree Hotel** Right **Oriental Spa, Oriental Hotel**

TOP 10 Spas

1 The Spa by MSpa

This sumptuous spa is comprised of two private suites and a variety of rooms, as well as a manicure and pedicure salon. The complex is designed in a blend of Lanna and Moroccan styles. *Four Seasons Hotel, Ratchadamri Road • Map Q3 • (02) 126 8866 • Open 10am–10pm daily • www.fourseasons.com/bangkok/spa*

The Spa by MSpa, Four Seasons Hotel

2 I. Sawan Residential Spa and Club

This luxurious spa, set amid the Grand Hyatt Erawan's lovely roof gardens, offers a wide range of treatments, each falling into one of four categories: Energy, Harmony, Purity, or Thai. *Grand Hyatt Erawan, 494 Ratchadamri Road • Map Q3 • (02) 254 1234 • Open 9am–11pm daily • www.bangkok.grand.hyatt.*

3 Banyan Tree Spa

Located on the 39th floor of the Banyan Tree Hotel, this deluxe spa has fantastic views and offers a variety of services including massages, scrubs, beauty treatments, and a bath menu. The Banyan Day package is a seven-hour marathon, which includes just about everything. *Banyan Tree Hotel, Sathorn Road • Map Q5 • (02) 679 1052–4 • Open 9am–10pm daily • www.banyantreespa.com*

4 Oriental Spa

This spa is an oasis of calm, combining ancient Asian healing philosophies with modern Western techniques. The traditional Thai teak building is the ideal place to unwind with a "jet-lag massage," a floral mask facial, or an Oriental mud wrap. *Oriental Hotel • Map M5 • (02) 659 9000 ext. 7440 • Open 9am–10pm daily • www.mandarinoriental.com*

5 Chi, The Spa

Based on the design of a Tibetan temple, this spa facility is nothing less than a sanctuary of tranquility. The wide array of treatments is designed to restore *chi*, a Chinese term that refers to the universal life force that governs well-being and personal vitality. Nine spacious treatment rooms offer sweeping river views and are equipped with an infinity bath, a herbal steam shower, and relaxation and changing areas. *Shangri-La Hotel • Map M6 • (02) 236 7777 • Open 10am–10pm daily • www.shangri-la.com/en/corporate/chi*

6 Oasis Spa at Sukhumvit 51

This day spa is set in lush tropical gardens and is tastefully decorated with teak furniture and cotton fabrics from Bali. The wide range of treatments on offer includes facials and massages, taken individually or as spa packages. Try the algae detoxifying body wrap or the signature Ultimate Body Massage.

Chi, The Spa

§ 88 Sukhumvit Soi 51
• Map T6 • (02) 262 2122 • Open 10am–10pm daily • www.bangkokoasis.com

The Grande Spa
Located at the five-star Sheraton, this spa has an excellent reputation. There is an extensive menu of treatments which combine the timeless wisdom of Thailand's healing arts with the very best of contemporary trends. § The Sheraton Grande Sukhumvit, 250 Sukhumvit Soi • Map T6 • (02) 649 8121 • Open 8am–10pm daily • www.sheratongrandesukhumvit.com

The Grande Spa

The Oasis Spa
This day spa facility is set in a huge garden which helps to create an aura of calm, with birds twittering in the trees outside the treatment rooms. Options provided by the spa include an Oasis Four Hands Massage, in which two masseurs work in unison, and the King of Oasis, which involves Thai and oil massages with hot compresses. § 64 Sukhumvit Soi 31 • Map T6 • (02) 262 2122 • Open 10am–10pm daily • www.bangkokoasis.com

Leyana Spa
This is another day spa set in a lush, tropical garden. It offers a dizzying array of treatments – massage, facial, body scrub, and body wrap, plus half-day and full-day packages. The body scrubs use tropical fruits such as tamarind and lemon, while the massage employs an aromatic blend of essential oils. § 33 Thonglor Soi 13 • Map T6 • (02) 391 7694 • Open 11am–10pm daily • www.leyanaspa.com

Spa I Am
A day spa located to the north of the city center, this large facility has 20 treatment rooms, two hydrotherapy suites, a couple suite, a beauty room, a fitness room, and a snack bar. Treatments include stone therapy massage, mud body mask, and a face firming treatment. § 88 Ladprao Soi 18 • Map T4 • (02) 938 4888 • Open 10am–10pm daily • www.spaiam.co.th

Left **Bronze image of the Buddha, Wat Suthat** Center **Wat Bowoniwet** Right **Wat Benjamabophit**

Buddhist Temples

Wat Phra Kaeo
For many visitors, the highlight of their stay in Bangkok is a visit to Wat Phra Kaeo, to see beautiful examples of Buddhist art and architecture. It has a glittering array of *chedi*, libraries, mausoleums, and the small jadeite Buddha that is the nation's greatest treasure (see pp8–11).

Wat Pho
Bangkok's biggest and oldest temple, Wat Pho's main attraction is its 150-ft (46-m) long Reclining Buddha. This *wat* is more typical of temples countrywide than Wat Phra Kaeo because it has resident monks who live in simple lodgings within the complex. It also runs a respected school of massage (see pp14–15).

Wat Arun
The Temple of Dawn, or Wat Arun, is a striking Bangkok landmark. Its unusual design, with one huge central *prang* (tower) and four others around it, shows the strong influence of Khmer architecture. It enjoyed a spell of glory between 1767 and 1782, when it housed the Emerald Buddha before the statue was transferred to Wat Phra Kaeo. Wat Arun is best viewed at sunset from across the Chao Phraya River (see pp26–7).

Wat Mahathat
Prince Mongkut spent 24 years as a monk in Wat Mahathat, before he became Rama IV (see p34). Mahachulalongkorn Buddhist University and a meditation center are housed here.
Ⓢ *Mahathat Road • Map B3 • (02) 221 5999 • Open 7am–8pm daily*

Wat Benjamabophit
The last major temple to be built in Bangkok, this is more commonly referred to by Western visitors as the Marble Temple because of its Carrara marble *bot*. The cloisters contain over 50 Buddha images displaying a variety of *mudra* (hand gestures). The main Buddha image is a copy of the Phra Buddha Chinarat that resides in Phitsanulok in northern Thailand (see p90).

Wat Suthat
One of the most important temples in Thailand, Wat Suthat was built in the early 19th century to house the 26-ft (8-m) tall, bronze Buddha image from Sukhothai, which sits in the *wihan*, surrounded by colorful murals. The galleries around the *wihan* hold over 150 Buddha images. The towering Sao Ching Cha, or Giant Swing, once used in a Brahmin ceremony, stands in front of the temple (see p65).

The *bot*, Wat Arun

58

7 Wat Bowoniwet

Built in 1826, this temple has gained significance for being the place where Siamese and Thai kings are ordained and as the base of Buddhism in Thailand.
◈ 240 Phra Sumen Road • Map C2
• (02) 280 0869 • Open 8am–5pm daily
• www.watbowon.org

The Golden Mount near Wat Saket

8 Wat Saket and the Golden Mount

Built by Rama I in the late 18th century, this temple has some excellent murals and a peaceful atmosphere. The main reason people visit here is to climb the Golden Mount, a 250-ft (76-m) high man-made hill, to view the Old City landmarks *(see p64)*.

9 Wat Traimit

This temple compound looks rather ordinary, but it is firmly fixed on the tourist trail because of the Golden Buddha, a 10-ft (3-m) high Sukhothai-style image made of solid gold *(see p73)*.

10 Wat Ratchabophit

A blend of local and Western architecture, this temple was built in the late 19th century by Rama V *(see p34)*. Its 141-ft (43-m) *chedi* is surrounded by cloisters, into which are set a *wihan* and a *bot* designed like an Italian Gothic chapel. ◈ Fuang Nakhon Road • Map C4 • (02) 221 1888 • Open 5am–8pm daily; bot: open 9–9:30am, 5:30–6pm daily

Top 10 Elements of a Thai Temple Compound

1 Wihan
The main assembly hall where the head abbot gives sermons and people pray.

2 Bot
The ordination hall, which is usually smaller than the *wihan*. Highly decorated, it is off-limits to women.

3 Chedi
These dome-shaped religious monuments, or stupas, have relics sealed within their base.

4 Bodhi Tree
This tree (*Ficus religiosa*) symbolizes Enlightenment, as the Buddha was sitting beneath a Bodhi tree when he attained Nirvana.

5 Ho Trai
The library stores sacred texts and is often raised off the ground to avoid floods.

6 Guti
These are monks' living quarters, usually just a small wooden room on stilts.

7 Murals
Temple murals depict incidents from the life of the Buddha, and some record scenes of Thai daily life.

8 Buddha Images
Usually the most highly valued Buddha image is placed in the *wihan*. Others may sit or stand in the *bot* or cloisters.

9 Monks
Holy men who follow the Buddha's teachings and advise lay people on their problems.

10 Novices
Young men live as novices in the temple before being ordained as monks.

All Thai men are expected to join the monkhood at some point in their lives – usually for three months when they are 20 years old

59

AROUND TOWN

BANGKOK'S TOP 10

Left **Wat Pho** Center **Stairs to the Golden Mount** Right **Amulet from the Amulet Market**

Old City

BANGKOK'S HISTORICAL AND SPIRITUAL *heart lies in the Old City. When Chao Phraya Chakri, later pronounced Rama I, assumed the throne in 1782, he first had a canal dug across a neck of land on the east bank of the Chao Phraya River to create an island that emulated the former capital at Ayutthaya. This island became known as Rattanakosin, and these days it and the area to the east of it are known as the Old City. Here stand the Grand Palace, once home of the royal family, and Wat Phra Kaeo, a glittering temple that houses the Emerald Buddha, as well as several important temples, museums, universities, and Sanam Luang, a public area where, occasionally, royal events take place.*

Wat Saket

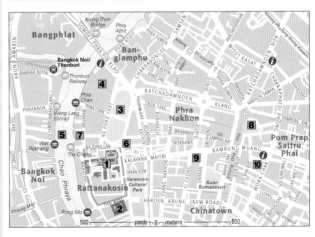

Preceding pages **M.R. Kukrit's Heritage Home**

Grand Palace and Wat Phra Kaeo

Located right in the center of Rattanakosin Island, the huge complex that contains the Grand Palace and Wat Phra Kaeo is one of Asia's unforgettable sights. It is the best place to get an introduction to Thai architecture and art. While the palace is strongly influenced by Italian Renaissance architecture, the temple complex is totally Thai, from the towering *bot* (ordination hall) that holds the Emerald Buddha to the slender lines of the Phra Si Rattana Chedi and the *Ramakien* murals that decorate the galleries on all sides *(see pp8–11)*.

Ramakien mural, Wat Phra Kaeo

Wat Pho

Officially known as Wat Phra Chetuphon, this is Bangkok's oldest and largest temple and a welcoming center of learning, particularly of the massage techniques for which it is famous. While Wat Phra Kaeo impresses visitors with its bejeweled monuments and glittering images, Wat Pho's charms are more subtle. Now under full renovation, it has a lively atmosphere and a dilapidated grandeur. Although the temple's main tourist attraction is the 150-ft (46-m) long Reclining Buddha, which fills a *wihan* (assembly hall) in the northwest corner of the compound, it can be just as much fun exploring quieter corners of the grounds and chatting with the resident monks, schoolchildren, and massage practitioners *(see pp14–15)*.

Sanam Luang

Considering Bangkok's congested streets and high-rise buildings crowded with people, it is amazing that a large open area such as Sanam Luang, or Royal Field, could exist at all. Its importance for certain royal ceremonies, such as cremation rites of royalty, guarantee that this precious patch of land will never be developed into offices or malls. From February to April, when the breeze allows, people fly kites here, and fortune tellers often ply their trade on the fringes of the field. ◈ *Na Phra Lan Road • Map B3*

National Museum

Located near the northern end of Rattanakosin Island, the National Museum *(see pp12–13)* is the repository of significant Thai art. The huge area it covers reflects the breadth and depth of Thai artistic achievement. Exhibits range from Dvaravati sculptures over 1,000 years old, to lavish funeral chariots, and the delightful Buddhaisawan Chapel, which houses the Phra Sihing Buddha image, second only in importance to the Emerald Buddha in Wat Phra Kaeo.

Dvaravati Wheel of Law, National Museum

Spirits in Thai Society

Lak Muang, the Amulet Market, and spirit houses (shrines dedicated to the spirit of the land on which a house is built) are all animist structures, which demonstrate that Thai religious belief is not limited to Buddhism. In fact, Buddhism's success here is partly due to its assimilation of aspects of other belief systems, such as Hinduism.

River and Canal Tour

Many visitors to Bangkok want to take a trip on the river and nearby canals to get a sense of how the city was before the advent of the motor car and catch a glimpse of traditional canal-side life. There are plenty of tours that are easy to organize through your hotel or guesthouse. Another option is to negotiate a price with a longtail-boat owner at any of the principal piers and arrange a customized tour *(see pp16–17)*.

Lak Muang

Lak Muang

This is the shrine that houses the city pillar of Bangkok, which was erected by Rama I in 1782 and is believed to contain the city's guardian spirit, Phra Siam Thewathirat. Also in the shrine is the city pillar of Thonburi, which is now part of Greater Bangkok. Both pillars are made of wood with lotus-shaped crowns and are painted gold. It is constantly busy with devotees, and there are sometimes performances of classical dance at the shrine, paid for by those grateful for good fortune. ◈ *Corner of Ratchadamnoen and Lak Muang roads • Map C4 • Open 8:30am–5:30pm daily*

Amulet Market

There is a strong belief among Thais that small images of the Buddha, famous kings, or even tigers' teeth worn as pendants can provide protection from misfortune. It is thus quite common to see people wearing a string of such amulets around the neck, and some even become ardent collectors of amulets. One of the best places to see this faith demonstrated is in the Amulet Market on the streets around Wat Mahathat. Potential buyers scrutinize the tiny objects with magnifying glasses and quiz the vendor to ascertain the amulet's properties. ◈ *Mahathat Road and small lanes • Map B4 • Open 8am–6pm daily*

Wat Saket and the Golden Mount

This was one of the first temples to be built when the city was founded in the late 18th century. Initially it served as a crematorium for the common people. Fine murals adorn the walls of the *wihan* (assembly hall). The main attraction here is to climb the 320 steps that lead to the summit of the Golden Mount, a 250-ft (76-m) high artificial hill surmounted by a golden, bell-shaped *chedi* (stupa), and witness fine views of the Old City skyline. The annual temple fair in November *(see p49)* features a candlelit parade to the summit. ◈ *344 Chakkaphatdi Phong • Map E3 (Wat Saket) and Map D3 (Golden Mount) • (02) 223 4561 • Open 8am–5:30pm daily • Adm (for Golden Mount)*

Wat Suthat

9 Wat Suthat

Begun in 1807 by Rama I (r.1782–1807) and completed by his successors, Wat Suthat is one of Bangkok's most important temples. Fronted by the towering Sao Ching Cha, a giant swing that was once used for a Brahmin ceremony, the compound has the tallest *wihan* in the city, especially constructed to accommodate the Phra Sri Sakyamuni Buddha, a 26-ft (8-m) tall 14th-century Sukhothai image. The murals in the *wihan* are beautifully detailed, and the temple grounds include four lovely bronze horses. ✪ *146 Bamrung Muang Road • Map D4 • (02) 224 9845 • Open 8:30am–9pm daily • Adm*

10 Soi Ban Baat

Monks have few material possessions – the *baat* (alms bowl) is one of them. Early each morning the bowls are filled with food offerings by devout Buddhists. They are mostly made in factories, but in Soi Ban Baat, or Monk's Bowl Village, there are still a few families that beat out the bowls by hand. Traditionally, these *baat* are made of eight strips of metal to represent the Eightfold Path of Buddhism. First, they are welded in a kiln, then shaped and filed smooth, and finally fired again. ✪ *Soi Ban Baat, Boriphat Road • Map D4*

A Stroll Through the Old City

Morning

🕐 Begin your exploration of the Old City at **Wat Saket**, where you can climb the **Golden Mount** to enjoy a wonderful, panoramic view of the area. From here walk south along Boriphat Road until you reach **Soi Ban Baat**, where alms bowls are beaten out of strips of metal. Go back up Boriphat Road, then left into **Bamrung Muang Road** *(see p66)* where shops sell Buddha images and temple paraphernalia. When you reach the unmissable **Sao Ching Cha**, turn into **Wat Suthat** and appreciate the superb carvings and paintings on display. Continue over the Klong and turn right onto **Sanam Chai** for the lush green lawns of **Sanam Luang**. For lunch, follow the road at the southern end of the park to a row of charming 19th-century shops and **Na Phra Lan Café** *(see p69)*, serving tasty Thai dishes.

Afternoon

After lunch, get back to Bamrung Muang Road, turn right and walk to the walls around **Wat Phra Kaeo** *(see pp8–11)*. Turn right again to reach the **Lak Muang** shrine and watch supplicants making offerings and praying. Wander west between **Sanam Luang** *(see p63)* and Wat Phra Kaeo, to view paintings at the **Silpakorn University Art Exhibition Hall** *(see p67)*. Buy yourself a lucky charm at the fascinating **Amulet Market** on Mahathat Road or along the small lanes off it. Carry on to the riverside pier and end the stroll with a cool drink at **S&P Restaurant** *(see p69)*.

Left **Detail of colorful tile, Wat Ratchabophit** Center **Phra Sumen Fort** Right **Wat Ratchanadda**

Best of the Rest

Wat Ratchabophit
The design of this temple is based on the *chedi* (stupa) at Nakhon Pathom *(see p98)*. The highlights include inlay work on the doors and windows of the *bot* (ordination hall) and colorful tiles in the cloisters *(see p59)*.

Bamrung Muang Road
Originally an elephant trail, this was one of the first roads to be paved in Bangkok. Its shops sell temple necessities such as monks' robes, candles, incense, and Buddha images. Ⓢ *Map D4*

Museum of Siam
Spread over three floors, this museum features fascinating interactive exhibits that explore Thai history and culture, Buddhism, and more. Ⓢ *Sanam Chai Road • Map J3 • (02) 225 2777 • Open 10am–6pm Tue–Sun & pub hols • Adm*

Wat Bowoniwet
The base of the Tammayut sect of Buddhism, this temple has some striking murals with unexpected themes, such as horse racing in England and Dutch windmills *(see p59)*.

Wat Mahathat
This temple is the headquarters of Mahachulalongkorn Buddhist University and home of the respected Vipassana Meditation Center *(see p58)*.

National Gallery
Located in a building that once housed the Royal Mint, this is Bangkok's principal art gallery. It features the work of established and emerging Thai artists. Ⓢ *4 Chao Fa Road • Map C3 • (02) 282 2639 • Open 9am–4pm Wed–Sun • Adm*

Khao San Road
Besides guesthouses, the backpacker's ghetto has souvenir shops, market stalls, and restaurants. Ⓢ *Map C3*

Phra Sumen Fort
This octagonal, brick-and-stucco fort was built in 1783 to defend the city from attack. Ⓢ *Phra Athit Road • Map C2*

Loha Prasat and Wat Ratchanadda
The Loha Prasat is a stepped pyramid with 37 spires on top of a metal palace. Its grounds are shared with Wat Ratchanadda. Ⓢ *2 Maha Chai Road • Map D3 • (02) 224 8807 • Open 8am–5pm daily*

King Prajadhipok (Rama VII) Museum
This state-of-the-art museum examines the events of 1925–35, which included the transition of Siam from absolute to constitutional monarchy. Ⓢ *2 Lan Luang Road • Map D3 • (02) 280 3413 • Open 9am–4pm Tue–Sun • Adm*

Left **Interior, Buddhaisawan Chapel** Center **Mahakan Fort** Right **Wat Mahathat meditation room**

🏆10 Ten Quiet Corners

1 Buddhaisawan Chapel, National Museum

After learning about Thai history in the National Museum, settle down on the cool teak floorboards of this lovely chapel to meditate, in front of the Phra Sihing Buddha image *(see p12)*.

2 Sanam Luang

This open grassy area has several benches in the shade of trees that offer rest to weary legs *(see p63)*.

3 Massage Pavilion, Wat Pho

Traditional Thai massage is a great remedy for aching legs and a muddled mind. The massage pavilion at Wat Pho has some of the best masseurs in the country *(see p14)*.

4 Saranrom Park

With shady trees, fountains, and benches, this park is a great place to take a break after trekking round the Grand Palace or Wat Pho. ⬡ *Rachini Road • Map C4 • (02) 221 0195 • Open 5am–9pm daily*

5 Santichaiprakhan Park

Looking out over the Chao Phraya River, this park makes an excellent place to sit and see the world go by. You also have the option to join the aerobics class held here at dusk every day. ⬡ *Phra Athit Road • Map C2 • Open 5am–10pm daily*

6 Corrections Museum, Romaninart Park

Formerly the site of a prison, this park now has ponds, fountains, shaded paths, and a museum which displays instruments of punishment. ⬡ *Maha Chai Road • Map D4 • (02) 226 1704 • Open 5am–9pm daily*

7 Silpakorn University Art Exhibition Hall

Tucked away inside the country's leading art school, this tranquil gallery features works by teachers, students, and artists-in-residence at the university. ⬡ *Na Phra Lan Road • Map B4 • (02) 221 3841 • Open 9am–7pm Mon–Fri*

8 Mahakan Fort

This octagonal fort has a park beside it, which is a great place for relaxation. ⬡ *Maha Chan and Ratchadamnoen roads • Map D3*

9 Riverside Restaurants, Tha Maharat

The cool river breeze makes this restaurant terrace beside Tha Maharat one of the best places to recover from a tiring walk. ⬡ *Mahathat Road • Map B3*

10 Meditation Room, Wat Mahathat

This venerable temple offers meditation courses in morning and afternoon sessions. ⬡ *Mahathat Road • Map B3 • (02) 222 6011 • Open 6:30am–9pm daily*

Around Town – Old City

Left **Gulliver's Traveler's Tavern** Center **Deep** Right **Molly 31**

Bars and Clubs

Gulliver's Traveler's Tavern
A typical Khao San Road bar, with everything a budget traveler needs – airconditioning, sports TV, international food, and extended happy hours. ✪ *Khao San Rd • Map C3 • (02) 629 1988 • Open 11am–2am daily • www.gulliverbangkok.com*

Boh
This bar has an excellent view across the Chao Phraya River to Wat Arun, making it a great spot for a sundowner. ✪ *230 Tha Thien • Map B5 • (02) 622 3081 • Open 5pm–1am daily*

Sabai Bar
With a decent menu, good location, and frequent 2-for-1 offers on beer, Sabai Bar does brisk business. ✪ *Sunset Street, 197 Khao San Rd • Map C3 • Open 6pm–2am daily*

Silk Bar
Khao San Road is going upscale, as exemplified by this swish bar with a good range of cocktails and well-prepared Thai food. ✪ *129–131 Khao San Rd • Map C3 • (02) 281 9981 • Open 8am–2am daily • www.silkbars.com*

Dickinson's Culture Cafe
Music starts here from about 6pm, with drum and bass, reggae, and dubstep. ✪ *64 Phra Athit Road • Map C2 • (089) 497 8422 • Open noon–1am Mon–Fri, 5pm–1am Sat & Sun*

The Club
A vast dance floor, a lively atmosphere, and music ranging from techno to trance pull in the crowds here. ✪ *123 Khao San Rd • Map C3 • (02) 629 2255 • Open 10pm–3am daily*

Brown Sugar: The Jazz Boutique
This long-established jazz bar, one of Bangkok's truly iconic night-time venues, attracts some exceptionally talented musicians. There is live music every night (see p42).

999 West
In the heart of the Khao San backpacker area is this Wild West saloon-style bar, with lively DJs and live bands. ✪ *108/5-6 Rambuttri Road • Map C2 • (02) 629 3992 • Open 11am–2am daily*

Deep
This club has both chill-out and dance areas, with live acoustic music as well as rock and drum and bass DJs. ✪ *Rambuttri Road • Map C2 • (02) 629 4260 • Open 5pm–2am daily*

Molly 31
In a renovated colonial-style building, this classy bar and club has a live band on the ground floor and a DJ upstairs. ✪ *146 Rambuttri Road • Map C3 • Open 11am–1am daily*

Price Categories

For a meal for one made up of one or two dishes served with a soft drink and including service.

B	under B100
BB	B100–200
BBB	B200–500
BBBB	B500–1,000
BBBBB	over B1,000

Above **May Kaidee**

🔟 Restaurants

1 Krisa Coffee Shop
Krisa is an ideal place for a light Thai lunch and a refreshing cold drink before or after a visit to the Grand Palace. ◈ *Na Phra Lan Road • Map B4 • (02) 225 2680 • Open 10:30am–6pm daily • BB*

2 May Kaidee
This restaurant serves some delicious and cheap vegetarian dishes. It has been so successful that it has now opened its own cookery school. ◈ *59 Tanao Road • Map C3 • (02) 629 4413 • Open 9am–11pm daily • www.maykaidee.com • B*

3 Na Phra Lan Café
Nestled amid shops opposite the Grand Palace, this café serves delicious fruit juices and Thai and Western dishes. ◈ *Na Phra Lan Road • Map B4 • (02) 221 2312 • Open 10:30am–10:30pm Mon–Sat, 10:30am–6pm Sun • B*

4 S&P, Maharat Pier
Part of a countrywide chain of restaurants, S&P turns out tasty Thai food, ice creams, and cakes. This branch has a breezy riverside terrace. ◈ *Maharat Pier • Map B3 • Open 10am–10pm daily • BB*

5 Somsong Pochana
Traditional Sukhothai-style noodles are served at this excellent little lunch spot. ◈ *112 Soi Wat Sangwet, near Phra Sumen Fort • Map C2 • Open 9:30am–4pm daily • B*

6 Hemlock
A small, trendy café, Hemlock offers a huge menu with many unusual dishes, including several vegetarian options. ◈ *56 Phra Athit Road • Map B2 • (02) 282 7507 • Open 5:30–11pm daily • BB*

7 Rub Aroon
This small shophouse has inside and outside seating, a varied menu of staple Thai dishes, and plenty of drinks. ◈ *Maharat Road • Map B5 • (02) 622 2312 • Open 10am–7pm daily • BB*

8 Kaloang Home Kitchen
Hidden behind the National Library, this simple, alfresco riverside venue serves excellent, inexpensive Thai cuisine. ◈ *2 Soi Wat Tevarakunchorn • Map C2 • (02) 281 9228 • Open 11am–10pm daily • BBB*

9 Roti Mataba
This restaurant specializes in Southern Thai dishes such as *roti mataba*, a delicious stuffed pancake that makes for an excellent lunch. ◈ *Corner of Phra Athit and Phra Sumen roads • Map C2 • (02) 822 2119 • Open 7am–8pm daily • BB*

10 Tom Yam Kung
Named for Thailand's signature dish, a sour and spicy shrimp soup, Tom Yam Kung has an extensive menu. ◈ *Khao San Rd • Map C3 • (02) 629 1818 • Open 11am–1am daily • BBB*

Left **Chinese lanterns on sale** Right **Busy Chinatown streets**

Chinatown

AT THE TIME OF BANGKOK'S FOUNDING *in 1782 (see p34), Chinese immigrants were moved out of Rattanakosin Island to make way for the Grand Palace and government buildings. They settled in the region to the south of Rattanakosin Island beside the Chao Phraya River. These days Chinatown is one of the most colorful and congested areas of the city, and though it lacks the grand monuments of the Old City, it is fascinating to take a stroll through its maze of alleys, passing markets, gaudy temples, and gleaming gold shops. Sharing this crowded part of the capital with the Chinese is a small community of Indians in a sub-district known as Little India, with the cloth market of Phahurat at its heart. East of Phahurat, Sampeng Lane was once a hot-bed of opium dens, brothels, and pawn shops. Today its shops sell household goods and fashion accessories.*

🔟 Sights

1. **Golden Buddha, Wat Traimit**
2. **Pak Khlong Market**
3. **Phahurat Market (Little India)**
4. **Hua Lampong Station**
5. **Yaowarat Road**
6. **Songwat Road**
7. **Nakorn Kasem Market**
8. **Wat Mangkon Kamalawat (Wat Leng Noi Yee)**
9. **Sampeng Lane**
10. **Talad Kao and Talad Mai**

Vendors selling chilies, Pak Khlong Market

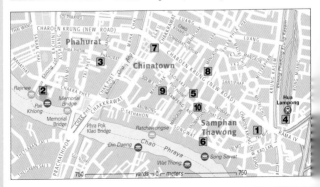

Preceding pages **Buddhaisawan Chapel, National Museum**

Golden Buddha, Wat Traimit

Golden Buddha, Wat Traimit

There are thousands of gold-leaf smothered Buddha images in Thailand, but what makes the Golden Buddha unique is that it is made of solid gold – all 12,000 lb (5,500 kg) of it. The true nature of the image was revealed only in 1955 when it was accidentally dropped, cracking the stucco surface to expose its gold interior. Housed in an otherwise unremarkable temple, this 13-ft (4-m) tall, 13th-century Sukhothai Buddha seems to glow with an inner light, making a visit worthwhile. ◎ *661 Charoen Krung Road • Map F6 • (02) 225 9775 • Open*

Pak Khlong Market

The onslaught of sights, sounds, and smells at Bangkok's biggest flower, vegetable, and fruit market threatens to cause sensory overload at any time of day or night. Throughout the night, boats laden with jasmine, lotus, and carnations unload their cargo, and at dawn the colorful displays of blooms and tropical fruits are at their best. The market is busiest in the mornings. ◎ *Chakphet Road • Map C5 • Open 24 hours daily*

Phahurat Market (Little India)

Crossing the road in Bangkok's Chinatown can seem like traveling from China to India in the blink of an eye. An enclave within an enclave, Little India, which is mostly concentrated along Phahurat Road and the block to the south, shows that Indians and Chinese share a love of commerce. Saris and rainbow-colored bolts of cloth are stacked to the rooftops of the cramped shophouses and spill out onto the narrow streets. Tiny teahouses and shops selling offerings for Hindu temples complete the whole scene. ◎ *Phahurat Road • Map C5 • Open 9am–6pm daily*

Hua Lampong Station

Initiated by Rama V (*see p34*), Hua Lampong Station was built just before World War I by Dutch architects, and though it has been modernized several times since then, the basic shell remains unchanged, making this train station one of Bangkok's most easily recognizable landmarks. This is the place where many out-of-towners begin their big city experience as they arrive at the railroad terminal and are more often than not preoccupied with avoiding scams rather than admiring the station's vaulted roof or mural paintings. ◎ *Rama IV Road • Map F6 • (02) 225 6964*

Hua Lampong Station

Yaowarat Road

5 The heart of Chinatown's gold trade, Yaowarat Road has over 100 gold shops along it. Painted bright red, these shops flaunt their displays of glittering necklaces and bracelets. On this one-way street the high volume of vehicles often makes traffic come to a complete halt, and each evening the street gets even busier as foodstalls and vendors occupy every square inch of space available. ✆ *Map E5*
• *Shops open 8am–10pm daily*

Songwat Road

6 Songwat Road runs parallel to the Chao Phraya River, and though the riverside piers and wharves are less busy now than a century ago, many companies still have their warehouses in this area, especially those in the rice trade. A stroll along this road and the small lanes that lead down to the river conjures up

Old wooden warehouse, Songwat Road

something of the atmosphere of Chinatown in bygone days, with tumbledown houses and cavernous warehouses lining the road. At its western end, Songwat Road leads to Pak Khlong, the flower market. ✆ *Map E6*

Nakorn Kasem Market

7 This market is still popularly known as "Thieves' Market" due to the dubious origin of many of the goods that were once sold here. In the mid-20th century this was a treasure trove for collectors of ancient Asian art and sculpture, including the famous Jim Thompson (*see pp24–5*). These days the market's offerings are much more prosaic, such as second-hand cooking utensils, electronic parts, and used stereo equipment. Although foreign visitors are unlikely to find much use for the items on sale, a walk through the market's narrow lanes can be great fun. ✆ *Corner of Charoen Krung and Chakkrawat roads*
• *Map D5* • *Open 9am–6pm daily*

Wat Mangkon Kamalawat (Wat Leng Noi Yee)

8 Established in 1871, this is the most important of Chinatown's many Chinese temples. Wat Mangkon Kamalawat, or Dragon Flower Temple, is particularly active during the Vegetarian Festival in October, when devotees flock here to make offerings. Also known as Wat Leng Noi Yee, it has an impressive entrance gateway and the complex contains Buddhist, Taoist, and Confucian shrines. It is constantly busy with people making offerings, and vendors selling religious goods outside the temple do a brisk business. ✆ *Charoen Krung Road* • *Map E5* • *(02) 222 3975*
• *Open 8am–6pm daily*

Sampeng Lane

9 This narrow lane, also known as Soi Wanit 1, stretches for about half a mile (1 km) through the very heart of Chinatown and embodies the frenetic commercial spirit of the district, but it is not for the faint-hearted. Cars cannot even squeeze their way down here, but motorbikes and porters carrying stacks of goods try to weave through the slow-moving sea of humanity. People pause every few steps to examine the goods on offer. These include computer games, fashion accessories, toys, ceramics, fabrics, and readymade garments.

Ⓢ Map L3 • Open 8am–8pm daily

Busy foodstalls, Sampeng Lane

Talad Kao and Talad Mai

10 These are both fresh-produce markets piled high with fish, mushrooms, mangoes, curry pastes, Chinese herbs, and spices. The Talad Kao, or Old Market, has been open for trade since the late 18th century, while the Talad Mai, or New Market, is about 100 years old. Together, they have earned themselves a good name for high-quality meat, fish, vegetables, and fruits. They remain particularly busy during the Chinese New Year. The old market is frantic at dawn, but winds down before lunchtime, while the new one continues to operate until evening.

Ⓢ Soi Isara Nuphap • Map E6 • Talad Kao: open 4–11am daily; Talad Mai: open 4am–6pm daily

Exploring Chinatown and Little India

Morning

🕘 Traffic can be a nightmare at any time in Chinatown, so take the public ferry to Tha Rachini, at around 9am. Take the first right on leaving the pier, cross the canal and go right again into **Pak Khlong Market** (see p73), which should be at its busiest and best at this time. Next, head north up Atsadang Road and then turn right into Phra Phitak Road. Within a couple of short blocks this becomes Phahurat Road, and you are transported to **Little India** (see p73). Keep walking straight through until you reach Chak Phet Road. Have a delicious north Indian lunch at the **Royal India** (see p77).

Afternoon

With batteries recharged, plunge into **Sampeng Lane** with its kitsch gadgets and wind-up toys. Make sure that your wallet or purse is well hidden as this is a pickpocket's paradise. When you reach Soi Isara Nuphap, turn left and wander past Chinese herbalists and pharmacists on your way to **Yaowarat Road**. Turn right here and notice the profusion of gold shops, all painted bright red with gold lettering, and most with an armed guard on duty. Where Yaowarat Road meets Charoen Krung Road, cross to the north side of the street and enter the temple of **Wat Traimit** (see p73). Sit down to rest and admire the superb crafts-manship of the **Golden Buddha** (see p73) and enjoy a tranquil end to the day.

Left **Flowers** Center **Spices** Right **Lanterns**

🔟 What to Buy

1 Flowers
Pak Khlong Market *(see p73)* is the place to buy fresh flowers – either individual cut blooms or a bouquet mixing a few favorites. Temperate flowers such as roses mingle with orchids and lotus ginger.

2 Gold
If you are seeking some gold ornamentation, check out the gold shops along Yaowarat Road *(see p74)*, which sell 23-carat gold in a variety of designs.

3 Textiles
The fantastic range of textiles on sale in Chinatown, and particularly in Phahurat Market *(see p73)*, is enough to tempt many visitors to take home a bolt of cloth or some inexpensive ready-made garments.

4 Incense
For the Chinese, incense is essential, particularly for making offerings, and several shops in Chinatown sell incense in coils, pyramids, small sticks, and big sticks that burn for hours.

5 Tea
Green tea and black tea, loose or packaged, is sold throughout Chinatown, and is consumed in great quantities by the Chinese themselves. Fresh markets and herbalists would be the best places for you to sniff out a good brew.

6 Fashion Accessories
There is nothing exclusive about the cheap trinkets on sale throughout Chinatown, particularly along Sampeng Lane *(see p75)*. Plastic earrings, strings of beads, cuddly mobile phone covers, and sequined handbags are a few of the items on offer.

7 Ceramics
Most of the ceramics on sale in Chinatown are functional rather than decorative, yet the ceramic shops are worth nosing around for unexpected treasures.

8 Lanterns
In a few of the narrow alleys off Soi Isara Nuphap there are families that still make traditional Chinese lanterns for a living. Shops along Sampeng Lane sell the finished product in a range of bright colors.

9 Spices
Head to any of the fresh markets in Chinatown to see colorful chili pastes and spices overflowing from huge enamel basins and pick out a few to experiment with back home.

10 Temple Offerings
The most common temple offerings are incense and colored paper, though shops specializing in religious necessities in Chinatown also sell miniature shrines and bright robes to drape around Chinese deities.

Price Categories

For a meal for one made up of one or two dishes served with a soft drink and including service.

B	under B100
BB	B100–200
BBB	B200–500
BBBB	B500–1,000
BBBBB	over B1,000

Above *Dim sum* ready to be served at Shangri La

TOP 10 Restaurants and Cafés

1 Nai Sow
This Chinese-Thai restaurant serves *tom yam kung*, a sour and spicy shrimp soup, as well as a host of stir-fries. ◉ *3/1 Maitri Chit Road • Map E5 • (02) 222 1539 • Open 10am–10pm daily • BB*

2 Royal India
In a back alley and scoring low on decor, Royal India serves great north Indian dishes. ◉ *392/1 Chak Phet Road • Map D5 • (02) 221 6565 • Open 10am–10pm daily • BBB*

3 Samrat
A Sikh-run eatery, Samrat prepares tasty curries, along with a small range of desserts and drinks. ◉ *Chak Phet Road • Map C5 • Open 9am–9pm daily • BB*

4 Shangri La
One of several in a chain of successful Cantonese restaurants, this huge place serves great *dim sum*, soups, and stir-fries. ◉ *306 Yaowarat Road • Map E5 • (02) 224 5807 • Open 10am–10pm daily • BBB*

5 Hua Seng Hong
Famed for its bird's nest soup, Hua Seng Hong offers other tasty alternatives such as *hoy tawt* (mussels in batter). ◉ *371–73 Yaowarat Road • Map E5 • (02) 222 0635 • Open 10am–midnight daily • BBB*

6 T & K
This restaurant specializes in barbecued seafood. ◉ *49 Soi Phadungdao • Map E6 • (02) 223 4519 • Open 4:30pm–2am daily • BBB*

7 White Orchid Hotel
The Chinese restaurant in this three-star hotel is famed for its *dim sum*, of which there is a fantastic range. The buffet lunch is a good deal too. ◉ *409–21 Yaowarat Road • Map E6 • (02) 226 0026 • Open 11am–2pm and 5–10pm daily • BBBB*

8 Chong Tee
Like many small eateries in Chinatown, Chong Tee specializes in one particular dish – pork satay served with sweet toast. ◉ *84 Soi Sukon, Trimitr Road • Map F6 • Open 10am–8pm daily • BB*

9 Food Center, Old Siam Plaza
The food court on the third floor of Old Siam Plaza serves a good range of Thai and Chinese dishes, while stalls on the first floor sell Thai desserts. The building is also a welcome escape from the heat. ◉ *Corner of Phahurat • Map C5 • Open 10am–5pm daily • BB*

10 Hong Kong Noodles
It is sometimes difficult to find a spare seat in this popular restaurant specializing in roast duck noodles. ◉ *136 Soi Isara Nuphap • Map E5 • Open 10am–8pm daily • BB*

Left **M. R. Kukrit's Heritage Home** Right *T'ai chi* practice at Lumphini Park

Downtown

THE DOWNTOWN AREA OF BANGKOK *radiates out eastwards from the Old City and Chinatown. It is a densely built-up area that includes embassies and business offices as well as the city's top hotels, restaurants, and entertainment venues. There are a few historical sights, including the Assumption Cathedral, and some gorgeous traditional houses, which contrast starkly with the surrounding skyscrapers. The lush Lumphini Park provides an escape from the concrete jungle, while Silom Road, Siam Square, and Ploenchit are the best shopping areas. Silom is also one of the city's liveliest areas for nightlife; along its infamous side streets, Patpong 1 and 2, market stalls and bars featuring live bands compete with go-go bars for visitors' attention.*

Jim Thompson's House

Beautiful interior of the Assumption Cathedral

🔟 Sights

1. Oriental Hotel
2. Assumption Cathedral
3. Jim Thompson's House
4. Erawan Shrine
5. Lumphini Park
6. Suan Pakkad
7. M.R. Kukrit's Heritage Home
8. Patpong
9. Snake Farm
10. Siam Square

Chef preparing food at the Oriental Hotel

Oriental Hotel

Bangkok's oldest hotel, the Oriental, enjoys double billing as both a historic sight and a luxurious accommodation option. It has hosted several famous writers, including Joseph Conrad and Somerset Maugham, in the Authors' Wing. This original part of the hotel, built in 1876, is now dwarfed by the Garden Wing and River Wing, but the oldest wing's fame still attracts visitors for a sundowner on its riverside terrace or a pot of tea in the Authors' Lounge. ◈ 48 Oriental Avenue • Map M5 • (02) 659 9000 • www.mandarinoriental.com/bangkok

Assumption Cathedral

Nestled in quiet backstreets near the riverside, this imposing building, erected in 1910, replaced a structure from the 1820s. It dominates a tree-lined square, which is part of a Catholic mission. An elaborately decorated pink and white exterior matches the brightly painted Rococo interior. The cathedral bears testimony to the success of French missions to Bangkok in the 19th century. While they made few conversions, they managed to secure religious tolerance for all. ◈ Soi Oriental • Map M6 • (02) 234 8556 • Open 6am–7pm daily

Jim Thompson's House

One of Bangkok's most popular sights, this beautiful compound of traditional Thai houses set in a lush tropical garden allows visitors to imagine how life in a well-to-do, early-20th century Bangkok home might have been. The evocative sculptures, tapestries, and furnishings inject the building with a refined character, and there is plenty of opportunity to linger, browsing silks in the shop, checking out the art gallery, and relaxing in the pondside café. Visitors must join a guided tour, which are regular and in several languages (see pp24–5).

Erawan Shrine

An island of spirituality in a sea of commerce, the Erawan Shrine is one of Bangkok's quirkiest sights, with the Skytrain zipping by and shopping malls hemming it in. Thailand's most famous spirit house gained its fame in 1956 when its installation was credited with halting a string of fatal accidents at the construction site of the former Erawan Hotel. A constant stream of supplicants offer marigolds, incense, and candles, along with silent wishes. Traditional dances are performed here on occasions when a supplicant's prayers are answered. ◈ Corner of Ratchadamri and Ploenchit roads • Map Q3

Offerings at the Erawan Shrine

Bangkok Traffic

Traffic in Bangkok is notorious for going nowhere. Drivers sit trapped in a sea of vehicles. Yet it was not always like this. In *The Land of the White Elephant* (1873), Frank Vincent writes: "the nobles...may occasionally be seen taking a drive at the fashionable hour of the afternoon, sitting gravely upright and... looking upon their friends...with a sense of new-found importance."

Lumphini Park

It is difficult to imagine how Bangkok might be without this green lung that occupies a huge block in the heart of the commercial and entertainment district. Consisting of a large lake, well-tended lawns, and shady trees, it is busy from dawn with locals walking, jogging, and performing *t'ai chi* in groups. There is a picnic area, snack bar, toilets, and even a bustling weight-lifting area at weekends. From February to April, it is a popular site for kite-flying.
Corner of Ratchadamri and Rama IV roads • Map Q4 • Open 5am–8pm daily

Suan Pakkad

This compound of traditional houses was assembled in the 1950s by Prince and Princess Chumbhot on land once used for farming vegetables (the name means "cabbage patch"). The compound has a varied collection of statues, paintings, porcelain, khon theater masks, and musical instruments. The highlight is the Lacquer Pavilion, which was brought here from a temple compound near Ayutthaya. *352–354 Sri Ayudhya Road • Map Q1 • (02) 246 1775–6 • Open 9am–4pm daily • Adm • www.suanpakkad.com/main_eng.php*

M.R. Kukrit's Heritage Home

Descended from Rama II (r.1809–24), Mom Rajawongse Kukrit Pramoj (1911–95) was one of the best-known and best-loved Thais of the 20th century. He founded the newspaper *Siam Rath* and wrote hundreds of plays, poems, and novels, including the popular epic *Four Reigns*, and even served as Prime Minister for a short spell in 1974–5. His house, with many beautiful artworks and a garden, has been preserved as he left it. *Soi 7, Narathiwat Ratchanakarin Road • Map P6 • (02) 286 8185 • Open 10am–4pm daily • Adm*

Patpong

Named for a Chinese millionaire who first started to develop these narrow lanes, Patpong 1 and 2 became world famous when their go-go bars began to be visited by US soldiers on leave from Vietnam in the late 1960s. Patpong's heyday was in the 1980s during Thailand's first tourist boom. In the early 1990s, a tourist night market was set up the whole length of Patpong 1, and the raunchy nightlife began to decline. The market is good for souvenir and fake goods shopping; the downstairs bars include live music cafés and loud go-go bars. Exercise normal caution at these places but take clear note that many upstairs bars are rip-off joints. *Between Silom and Surawong roads • Map P5 • Markets and bars open 6pm–1am daily*

Suan Pakkad compound

Snake Farm

9 One of Bangkok's quirkier attractions, the snake farm is located in the Queen Saovabha Memorial Institute, which was set up in 1923 as the Pasteur Institute. Now run by the Thai Red Cross, it produces serums for snake bites and promotes education about dangerous snakes. Daily programs include slide shows that explain how to treat a snake bite. During live demonstrations, snakes are milked of their venom and visitors are able to have a picture taken with the less harmful varieties. ⓢ *1871 Rama IV Road • Map P4 • (02) 252 0161 • Shows: 11am and 2:30pm Mon–Fri, 11am Sat–Sun • Adm*

Boutique, Siam Square

Siam Square

10 Flanked by multi-story shopping malls, Siam Square is a grid of streets packed with shopping arcades. The numerous tiny shops, some with no more than a meter frontage, make it a popular shopping area, especially for students from the neighboring Chulalongkorn University, who congregate around Center Point's milk bars and fast-food outlets at the southern end of the square. Juxtaposed with these cheap options are shops selling designer clothes and fashion accessories, the creation of enterprising young Thai designers. There is also a good selection of cafés and restaurants, plus multiplex cinemas. ⓢ *Corner of Rama I and Phaya Thai roads • Map P2*

A Walk Through the Old Farang Quarter

Morning

🕐 Begin this half-mile (1-km) walking tour at the **River City Shopping Complex** *(see p39)*, on the riverfront just north of the pier at Tha Si Phraya. This upscale shopping center offers jewelry, antiques, books, maps, clothes, and restaurants. On the third and fourth floor are shops selling rare antiques, and an antiques auction is held every fourth Saturday of the month. From here head back southwards, passing the **Royal Orchid Sheraton** to get a glimpse of the **Portuguese Embassy**. Operational from 1820, this was the first embassy to be established in Siam by any European power. Follow the lane out to Charoen Krung Road and turn right to reach the **General Post Office**, a massive Art Deco building. Walk south along Charoen Krung from the post office and turn right into Soi 34 to see old wooden houses; the winding lane leads to **Haroon Mosque**, a small, attractive stucco building used by the local Muslim population. Soi 36 brings you away from the river until you reach the **French Embassy**, the second embassy to be established in the city. Walk south, crossing Soi 38 and 40 to reach the **Assumption Cathedral** *(see p79)*. From the cathedral, follow an alley to the west towards the river, where the former headquarters of the East Asiatic Company, built in 1901, still stands. End the walk by stepping into the **Oriental Hotel** *(see p79)* next door, and having tea and cakes in the Authors' Lounge.

Left **Maha Uma Devi Temple** Center **Pratunam Market** Right **Royal Bangkok Sports Club**

Best of the Rest

1 Pratunam Market
Famous for its inexpensive clothes, Pratunam Market is a great place to witness Bangkok's chaotic street life. ✪ *Corner of Phetburi and Ratchaprarop roads • Map Q1 • Open 9am–midnight daily*

2 Baiyoke Tower II
Bangkok's tallest building at 1,000 ft (304 m), this tower has an open-air, revolving roof deck from where there are superb panoramas of the city. ✪ *222 Ratchaprarop Road • Map Q1 • (02) 656 3000 • Open 10:30am–10pm daily • Adm*

3 Maha Uma Devi Temple
Also known as Sri Mariamman, this temple features a panoply of brightly painted Hindu deities above the entrance and around the interior walls. ✪ *Corner of Silom Road and Soi Pan • Map N5 • (02) 238 4007 • Open 6am–8pm daily*

4 Royal Bangkok Sports Club
This horse-racing club, with a golf course set inside the track, looks very attractive from the Skytrain. ✪ *Henri Dunant Road • Map Q3 • (02) 255 1420 • www.rbsc.org*

5 Neilson Hays Library
Located in a colonial building, this haven for bookworms has over 20,000 volumes on its shelves. ✪ *195 Suriwong Road • Map N5 • (02) 233 1731 • Open 9:30am–5pm Tue–Sun*

6 Chao Mae Tubtim Shrine
This eye-catching shrine is surrounded by phallic offerings placed here by devotees wishing for fertility or prosperity. ✪ *Wireless Road • Map R2*

7 Robot Building
Headquarters of the United Overseas Bank, this modern building resembles a robot, complete with eyes and antennae. The building is best viewed from the elevated Skytrain. ✪ *South Sathorn Road • Map N6*

8 Siam Ocean World
A massive aquarium, home to over 400 species of marine life, featuring touch tanks, informative touch screens, and an underwater tunnel *(see p47)*.

9 Museum of Counterfeit Goods
Over 1,500 fake items are on display in this quirky museum, including clothing, footwear, electronics, car parts, and drugs. ✪ *Tilleke & Gibbins, 64 Soi Tonson, Ploenchit Road • Map R3 • (02) 263 7700 • Open 10am–4pm Mon–Fri*

10 Chulalongkorn University
Thailand's oldest and most respected university. Its campus mixes Western and Thai architectural styles. ✪ *254 Phaya Thai Road • Map P3 • (02) 215 0871 • www.chula.ac.th*

Left **Siam Paragon** Right **Siam Discovery Center**

🔝10 Shopping Malls

1 Siam Paragon
With six floors of designer boutiques, bookshops, cinemas, restaurants, and fitness centers, this mall is one of the most popular in Bangkok *(see p38).*

2 Siam Center and Siam Discovery Center
Known for designer brands, trendy shops, and restaurants, these adjoining malls attract young adults. Children love the Kids World in the Discovery Center. 🅢 *989 Rama I Road • Map P2 • (02) 658 1000 • Open 10am–10pm daily*

3 Mahboonkrong (MBK)
Packed with five floors of fashions and accessories, electronic goods, jewelry and cosmetics, as well as an excellent food court, Mahboonkrong (MBK) feels like a cross between a street market and a shopping mall *(see p38).*

4 Peninsula Plaza
This mall consists mostly of jewelers and designer outlets. 🅢 *153 Ratchadamri Road • Map Q3 • (02) 253 9791 • Open 10am–8pm daily*

5 CentralWorld
Huge shopping complex with fashion boutiques, jewelers, home decor outlets, a bowling alley, and cinemas. 🅢 *4/1–2 Ratchadamri Road*
• Map Q2 • (02) 640 7000
• Open 10am–10pm daily
• www.centralworld.co.th

6 Erawan Bangkok
Located next to the Erawan Shrine, this luxury mall has plenty of boutiques operated by famous names, as well as classy cafés and a wellness center. 🅢 *494 Ploenchit Road • Map Q3 • (02) 250 7777 • Open 10am–9pm daily • www.erawanbangkok.com*

7 Gaysorn Plaza
The focus here is on fashion, with many successful young Thai designers displaying their wares. There are also many home decor outlets *(see p39).*

8 H1
A boutique mall, H1 is geared to the top-end customer, with striking architecture and shops that are all design conscious. 🅢 *998/3 Sukhumvit 55 (Thonglor), Soi 38 • Map T6 • (02) 714 9578 • Open 10am–8pm daily*

9 Eight Thonglor
This boutique mall has three floors specializing in home decor and fashion outlets. 🅢 *88/36 Sukhumvit 55 (Thonglor) • Map T6 • (02) 714 9515 • Open 10am–10pm daily • www.8thonglor.com*

10 Emporium
An upscale mall, Emporium features a department store, designer boutiques, restaurants, and cafés. 🅢 *622 Sukhumvit Road • Map T6 • (02) 269 1000 • Open 10am–10pm daily*

Left **Riverside Terrace** Right **Shangri-La Horizon Cruise**

🔟 Hotel Buffets and Dinner Cruises

Colonnade Restaurant
With a casually elegant ambience, the Colonnade is a wonderful place to enjoy oysters or sushi at lunchtime or a fabulous spread of pan-Asian dishes in the evening. ⬧ *Sukhothai Hotel, 13/3 South Sathorn Road • Map Q6 • (02) 344 8888 • www.sukhothai.com • BBBBB*

Riverside Terrace
This place is tough to beat for its romantic location, and the evening buffet features grilled seafood and meats. ⬧ *Oriental Hotel, 48 Oriental Avenue • Map M5 • (02) 659 9000 • www.mandarinoriental. com/bangkok • BBBBB*

Dining Room
One of the city's best dinner buffets is served at the Dining Room, with roast carvings, pasta, and lots of fresh salads. ⬧ *Grand Hyatt Erawan, 494 Ratchadamri Road • Map Q3 • (02) 254 1234 • www.bangkok.hyatt.com • BBBBB*

Madison
Enjoy the special Sunday brunch at this luxury hotel restaurant. ⬧ *Four Seasons Hotel, 155 Ratchadamri Road • Map Q3 • (02) 126 8866 • www.fourseasons.com/ bangkok • BBBBB*

Next 2 Cafe
Serving all-day buffets, this restaurant by the river is especially good for Sunday brunch. ⬧ *Shangri-La Hotel, 89 Soi Wat Suan Phlu, Charoen Krug Road • Map M6 • (02) 236 7777 • www.shangri-la.com • BBBBB*

Loy Nava Cruise
Choose from traditional, seafood, and vegetarian Thai dishes, then sit back and enjoy the fare on this rice barge as it chugs up and down the Chao Phraya River. ⬧ *Si Phraya Pier • Map M5 • (02) 437 4932 • Cruise 6–8pm and 8–10pm • www.loynava.com • BBBBB*

Manohra Cruise
Operating out of the Anantara Bangkok Riverside, this cruise offers guests tasty curries and stir-fries. ⬧ *Anantara Bangkok Riverside Pier • Map S6 • (02) 476 0022 • Cruise 7:30–10pm • www.manohra cruises.com • BBBBB*

Pearl of Siam Cruise
This cruise is perfect for those looking for a lively evening. Boats are big and offer live music and lounge areas, plus a blowout buffet. ⬧ *River City Pier Complex • Map M5 • (02) 861 0255 • Cruise 7:30–9:30pm • www.grandpearlcruise.com • BBBBB*

Shangri-La Horizon Cruise
Step aboard this luxury river cruiser and sample some of the tastiest Thai dishes. Service is extremely attentive. ⬧ *Shangri-La Hotel Pier • Map M6 • (02) 236 7777 • Cruise 7:30–9:30pm • BBBBB*

Yok Yor Cruise
The only budget dinner cruise in Bangkok is popular but the menu is limited. ⬧ *885 Somdet Chaophraya 17 Road • Map L4 • (02) 863 0565 • Cruise 8–10pm • www.yokyor.co.th/ cruise/index.html • BBB–BBBB*

Price Categories

For a meal for one made up of one or two dishes, served with a soft drink and including service.

B	under B100
BB	B100–200
BBB	B200–500
BBBB	B500–1,000
BBBBB	over B1,000

Above **Le Normandie**

🔟 Restaurants

Le Normandie

The Brittany lobster and pan-fried duck liver are specialties of this French restaurant. ◈ *Oriental Hotel, 48 Oriental Avenue • Map M5 • (02) 659 9000 • Open noon–2:30pm Mon–Sat and 7–11pm daily • www. mandarinoriental.com/bangkok • BBBBB*

Sirocco

Situated half way to heaven, this is *the* place for a romantic Italian meal. ◈ *63rd floor, State Tower, 1055 Silom Road • Map M6 • (02) 624 9555 • Open 6pm–1am daily • BBBBB*

Breeze

The setting is spectacular, the seafood is impeccable, but the prices are steep at this high-rise restaurant. ◈ *52nd floor, State Tower, 1055 Silom Road • Map M6 • (02) 624 9555 • Open 6pm–1am daily • BBBBB*

Himali Cha Cha

Famous for its tandoori chicken, this cozy restaurant serves some of the best north Indian food in Bangkok. ◈ *1229/11 Charoen Krung Road • Map M5 • (02) 235 1569 • Open 11am–3:30pm and 6–10:30pm daily • BBB*

Angelini

This Italian eatery serves up a great antipasto lunch buffet. ◈ *Shangri-La Hotel, 89 Soi Wat Suan Plu, Charoen Krung Road • Map M5 • (02) 236 7777 • Open 6:30–10:30pm daily • BBBBB*

Tongue Thai

The curries and spicy salads are favorites at this early 20th-century converted shophouse. ◈ *18–20 Charoen Krung Soi 38 • Map M5 • (02) 630 9918–9 • Open 10:30am–2:30pm, 5:30–10:30pm daily • BB*

Eat Me

A very imaginative Australian/Pacific Rim menu is offered at this restaurant. ◈ *Soi Pipat 2, Convent Road • Map P5 • (02) 238 0931 • Open 3pm–1am daily • BBBBB*

Scarlett

This wine bar and French restaurant is on the 37th floor of the Sofitel Silom Hotel. Choose a bottle of wine and a "tasting tree" of tapas and enjoy the view. ◈ *188 Silom Road • Map N5 • (02) 238 1991 • Open 6pm–1am daily • BBBBB*

Fallabella

Set inside the Royal Bangkok Sports Club, Fallabella has great views and serves tasty dishes, such as *lasagna della casa* and Phuket lobster spaghetti as well as lamb cutlets. ◈ *100 Ratchadamri Road • Map Q4 • (02) 252 5131 • Open 11am–10pm daily • BBBBB*

Ban Khun Mae

With its extensive menu of classic Thai dishes, this is an ideal spot for lunch or dinner. ◈ *458/7–9 Siam Square Soi 8 • Map P2 • (02) 658 4112 • Open 11am–11pm daily • BBBB*

Left **Moon Bar** Right **Molly Malone's**

Bars and Pubs

Sky Bar

Indulge in a pricey sundowner at the Sky Bar and admire the view from near the top of the State Tower. ⍟ *63rd floor, State Tower, 1055 Silom Road • Map M6 • (02) 624 9555 • Open 6pm–1am daily*

The Zuk Bar

A relaxing place for a drink at the end of a hot day, The Zuk Bar bursts into life after 9pm, however, with resident DJs turning the heat back up. ⍟ *Sukhothai Hotel, 13/3 South Sathorn Road • Map Q5 • (02) 344 8888 • Open 5pm–1am Mon–Sat, noon–midnight Sun • www.sukhothaihotel.com*

Molly Malone's

A homely, two-story Irish sports bar with brass fittings and mahogany furnishings where expats get together to watch sports on TV. ⍟ *1 Convent Road • Map P5 • (02) 266 7160 • Open 9am–1am daily*

Bar@494

The excellent wines and tapas are reasonably priced at this small bar in the Grand Hyatt. ⍟ *Soi 6 Siam Square • Map Q3 • (02) 254 1234 • Open noon–midnight Mon–Sat, 5pm–midnight Sun*

For Fun Pub

This is a well-stocked bar and a good restaurant. A live band plays from 9pm. ⍟ *90–96 Silom Soi 4 • Map P5 • (02) 266 3682 • Open 8pm–2am daily*

Moon Bar

Enjoy the fabulous views from high up above the city at Moon Bar, which offers a complete range of cocktails. ⍟ *Banyan Tree Hotel, South Sathorn Road • Map Q6 • (02) 679 1200 • Open 5pm–1am daily*

O'Reilly's

The Irish theme here includes waitresses dressed in green, Guinness on tap, and Irish jigs played by the resident band. ⍟ *62/1-2 Silom Road • Map P5 • (02) 632 7515 • Open 10am–midnight daily*

Diplomat Bar

Unwind along with the high-flyers at this super-elegant bar while sipping a cocktail and enjoying the resident jazz band. ⍟ *Conrad Hotel, All Seasons Place, 87 Wireless Road (Witthayu) • Map R3 • (02) 690 9999 • Open 7am–1am Sun–Thu, 7am–2am Fri & Sat*

My Bar

Comfortable armchairs and bright decor give this bar a welcoming feel. ⍟ *Dusit Thani Hotel, 946 Rama IV Road • Map Q5 • (02) 200 9000 extn. 2999 • Open 5pm–1am daily*

Syn Bar

An intriguing mix of retro and futuristic design, this bar offers unusual cocktails such as mangosteen martini. ⍟ *Swissotel Nai Lert Park, 2 Wireless Road • Map R2 • (02) 253 0123 • Open 9am–1am daily*

Left **Interior of a bar in Bangkok** Center **Hard Rock Café** Right **Tapas**

TOP 10 Nightclubs and Music Venues

1 WOOBAR®

A wide variety of sounds, from techno to funky house, are played at this beautifully sophisticated hotel bar. ⊗ *W Bangkok Hotel, 106 Sathorn Nua • Map P6 • (02) 344 4000 • Open 9am–1am Sun–Wed, 9am–2am Thu–Sat*

2 Bamboo Bar

One of Bangkok's best spots for jazz lovers, Bamboo Bar has an excellent resident band, an elegant tropical atmosphere, and attentive waitresses who keep the drinks flowing (see p42).

3 Hard Rock Café

With a formula that has been tried and tested worldwide, Hard Rock Café is one of the liveliest night spots in Bangkok (see pp42–3).

4 Lucifer

Located amid the notorious Patpong bars, this disco with a devilish theme attracts plenty of punters as the night wears on (see p43).

5 Party House One

This bar and restaurant features different styles of music throughout the week – blues, electro jazz, swing, and lounge. ⊗ *865 Rama I Road, opposite National Stadium • Map N2 • (02) 217 3070 • Open 6pm–midnight daily*

6 Niu's On Silom

Live jazz, blues, and soul are served up here with some of the best Italian cuisine in town. ⊗ *661 Silom Road • Map N6 • (02) 266 5333 • Open 5pm–1am daily*

7 Tapas

Popular among the Bangkok party crowd, Tapas is *the* place to spot celebrities and be seen yourself. ⊗ *114/17 Silom Soi 4 • Map P5 • (02) 234 4737 • Open 7pm–2am daily • Adm*

8 DJ Station

Silom Soi 2 is dominated by gay clubs, and this three-floor nightclub is the most popular. ⊗ *Silom Soi 2 • Map P5 • (02) 266 4029 • Open 10pm–2am daily • Adm*

9 Concept CM²

The entertainment zones here include a main arena with live bands, the Boom Room where DJs mix up R&B, a huge karaoke lounge, and a sports bar. ⊗ *Basement, Novotel, Siam Square Soi 6 • Map P2 • (02) 209 8888 • Open 9pm–2am daily • Adm*

10 Mixx Discotheque

Known for its superb acoustics and sound system, this club plays hip-hop, R&B, and house music. ⊗ *President Tower Arcade, 973 Phloen Chit Road • Map Q2 • (02) 656 0382 • Open 10pm–2am daily • Adm*

Left **Figurehead on a barge, Royal Barge Museum** Right **Siriraj Hospital Museums**

Greater Bangkok

*S*INCE THE CITY WAS FOUNDED IN 1782, *it has gradually increased in size and today Greater Bangkok stretches at least 12 miles (20 km) north to south and east to west. Though most of the suburban areas are housing estates, a must-see for many visitors is Chatuchak Weekend Market, a shopper's paradise. Thonburi, the former capital to the west of the Chao Phraya River, has the enigmatic Wat Arun, the Royal Barge Museum, and some quirky museums in Siriraj Hospital. Dusit, to the north of the Old City, features the magnificent Dusit Park (see pp18–19) and the gleaming Wat Benjamabophit. To the east of the city lie Kamthieng House and the Rama IX Royal Park, while a short boat ride north, Nonthaburi and Koh Kret offer a taste of provincial Thailand.*

Nonthaburi Pier

Interiors, Kamthieng House

🔟 Sights

1. Chatuchak Weekend Market
2. Wat Arun
3. Siriraj Hospital Museums
4. Royal Barge Museum
5. Wat Benjamabophit
6. Phayathai Palace
7. Kamthieng House
8. Rama IX Royal Park
9. Nonthaburi
10. Koh Kret

Antiques stall at Chatuchak Weekend Market

1 Chatuchak Weekend Market

Originally located at Sanam Luang in the Old City, this market moved out to the northern suburbs in 1982. It now covers a massive area where somewhere between 10 and 15 thousand stalls sell a mind-boggling range of products, from antiques and paintings to plants and animals. Considered to be the world's largest open-air market, it is too big to see everything in a day. So pick up a map at the entrance and target the areas that interest you *(see pp22–3)*.

2 Wat Arun

This ancient temple in Thonburi, on the west bank of the Chao Phraya River, is one of Bangkok's best-known icons with its five towering *prang* (towers). These *prang* are covered with broken shards of colorful porcelain that create an intriguing abstract pattern when viewed up close. The temple's *bot* (ordination hall) is also worth exploring, both for its murals and the exquisite Buddha image, which was apparently molded by King Rama II. Parts of the temple complex are closed to visitors for renovations until fall 2016 *(see pp26–7)*.

3 Siriraj Medical Museums

If you are at all squeamish, then these "attractions" are not for you. However, many people are curious enough to take the risk. Take your pick from the Anatomical Museum with its Siamese twins, the Prehistoric Museum's overview of evolution, the Pathological Museum's focus on diseases, the Parasitology Museum's fixation with tapeworms, the Museum of History of Thai Medicine, and the most popular, the Museum of Forensic Medicine, which displays preserved organs, skulls, and horrific images of crime scenes.
🕾 *Phrannok Road • Map A3 • (02) 419 7000 • Open 9am–4pm Mon–Fri • Free • www.si.mahidol.ac.th*

4 Royal Barge Museum

This display of elaborately decorated vessels offers a glimpse into the pageantry of the Thai monarchy. The barges are long, narrow crafts that are propelled by brightly bedecked oarsmen on rare ceremonial occasions. The principal barge on display, *Suphanahongse*, carries the King and Queen at such times. It is carved out of a single teak tree and its prow is adorned with a majestic golden swan.
🕾 *Khlong Bangkok Noi • Map A2 • (02) 424 0004 • Open 9am–5pm daily • Adm • www.nationalmuseums.finearts.go.th/ thaimuseum_eng/royalbarges/history.html*

Porcelain exterior, Wat Arun

Wat Benjamabophit

Commissioned by Rama V *(see p34)* and designed by his half-brother, Prince Naris and Italian architect Ercole Manfredi, this is a cruciform temple made of Italian marble. The *bot* (ordination hall) is particularly beautiful, with stained-glass windows, carvings on the window panels, and a golden Buddha image, beneath which are interred the ashes of Rama V.
Nakhon Pathom Road • Map E2 • (02) 282 7413 • Open 8am–5:30pm daily • Adm

Wat Benjamabophit

Phayathai Palace

Built in 1909 as a royal country retreat where the King and Queen conducted agricultural experiments, this palace is now engulfed by urban development. It has also served as an exclusive hotel and a radio station, but after the 1932 coup *(see p34)* it was commandeered by the military as a hospital (Phramongkutklao Hospital), which still functions around the palace today. The highlight of the palace is the Thewaratsaparom Throne Hall, which was used by Rama VI (r.1910–25), a keen playwright and actor, as a theater. It has beautifully carved pillars, balconies, and archways. The Phiman Chakri Throne Hall, with its cone-topped turret, is also visually striking. Ratchawithi Road • Map H1 • (02) 354 7660 extn. 93694 • Saturday tours 9:30am and 1:30pm • Free

Kamthieng House

This beautiful Lanna house began life in the mid-19th century as the home of the Nimman-heimin family in Chiang Mai, but was carefully dismantled and reconstructed on this site in 1962 when it was donated to the Siam Society, whose offices and library are also located here. Today it functions as an ethnological museum, with farming implements beneath the house, a multimedia display on the Thai belief in spirits, a typical rural kitchen, and a granary with an exhibition on rice-farming rituals. 131 Sukhumvit Soi 21 • Map T6 • (02) 661 6470–7 • Open 9am–5pm Tue–Sat • www.siam-society.org/heritage/kamthieng.html

Rama IX Royal Park

This is an ideal spot to head for when you need a break from Bangkok's relentless congestion. Though it takes a while to get to the park, on entering the 200 acre (81 hectare) site, the effort becomes worthwhile. The park was opened in 1987 to commemorate Rama IX's *(see p35)* 60th birthday, and contains a museum explaining the life and achievements of the king, a large lake with pedal boats, as well as beautifully landscaped grounds with several unusual plants that are clearly labelled. Sukhumvit Soi 103 • Map U6 • Open 5am–6pm daily • Adm

The Dreaded Durian

The durian, a most unusual fruit, arouses adoration and disgust in equal measure for its strong repelling smell and heavenly creamy taste. The spiky shell belies the soft yellow pods beneath it, cushioned by thick padding. The mushy texture and smooth, tangy taste take some getting used to, but once hooked there is no going back.

Nonthaburi

9 For a quick escape from downtown Bangkok, take the express ferry heading north from any pier in the center of the city and get off at the last stop in Nonthaburi. The town is typical of provincial Thailand, and the only significant historical monument is the Wat Chalerm Phra Kiet. The temple, located on the opposite bank of the river from the jetty, is a beautiful structure that was originally built by Rama III (r.1824–51). Intricate porcelain tilework on the doors and window frames of the *bot* (ordination hall) has been painstakingly restored. This region is famed for the superior quality of its smelly but interestingly tasty durian fruit.
⊗ *Nonthaburi Province • Map S4*

Koh Kret terra-cotta pots

Koh Kret

10 Combining a trip to Nonthaburi with an exploration of Koh Kret, an ox-bow island in a meander of the Chao Phraya River, makes for an enjoyable day. Hire a longtail boat from Nonthaburi to reach Koh Kret. The island is inhabited by the Mon people, who make terra-cotta pots for sale in markets in the city. There are no cars, so you can listen to the twitter of birds as you wander around the island, passing mango, papaya, and durian plantations, pausing to watch busy potters at work, and perhaps picking up a sample of their work. ⊗ *4 miles (7 km) N of Nonthaburi • Map S4*

Exploring Chatuchak and Thonburi

Morning

Start before 8am and make your way to Mo Chit Skytrain station for a good look round **Chatuchak Weekend Market** *(see pp22–3)* before it gets too hot and crowded. Pick up a map at the main entrance on the Phaholyothin Road and go straight ahead through the maze of stalls to the slender clocktower to orient yourself. Check out section 8 (handicrafts), wander through sections 9–15 (pets and accessories) before stocking up your wardrobe in sections 10–21 (clothing and footwear). As there are thousands of foodstalls, you can refuel whenever you get hungry or thirsty.

Afternoon

At midday, return to Mo Chit station and take the Skytrain to Saphan Taksin. From here, take an express ferry upriver to Tha Thien, then hop on one of the regular cross-river ferries to **Wat Arun** *(see pp 26–7)*. Take a good look at the bright ceramics on the *prang* (towers), and clamber up the steep steps of the central spire for a panoramic river view. Rest in a breezy riverside pavilion before taking the ferry back to Tha Thien, then an express ferry to Tha Phra Athit, followed by a tourist shuttle boat to the **Royal Barge Museum** *(see p89)*. Marvel over the intricate decoration of the other-worldly vessels on display here before heading back to your base. If peckish on the ride home, stop off at **Ton Bo**, an open-sided restaurant right beside Phra Athit Pier.

Left **Library, Wat Rakhang** Center **Turtles in the pond at Wat Prayun** Right **Prasart Museum**

Best of the Rest

Christian Churches
Near the riverbank in Dusit district are three churches built for resident foreigners: St. Francis Xavier Church with its mainly Vietnamese congregation, the Church of the Immaculate Conception established by French missionaries, and a small Cambodian Church.
🕲 S of Ratchawithi Road • Map S5

Thewet Flower Market
With its bright blooms, sweet scent in the air, and the friendly smiles of the vendors, this canalside market is an appealing place to explore. 🕲 Krung Kasem Road • Map D1 • Open 9am–6pm daily

Wat Indrawiharn
The main attraction of this temple tucked away in the back-streets of Dusit is the 105-ft (32-m) tall standing Buddha.
🕲 144 Wisut Kasat Road • Map D1
• (02) 281 1406 • Open 6am–6pm daily

Wat Rakhang
A little-visited temple, Wat Rakhang has a wooden scripture library behind the *bot* (ordination hall), where there are murals from the days when Rama I (r.1782–1809) lived here as a monk. 🕲 Soi Wat Rakhang • Map A4

Wat Kalayanamit
The country's largest indoor sitting Buddha at 50 ft (15 m) and the biggest bronze bell are both to be found here. 🕲 Soi Wat Kanlaya
• Map B6 • Open 8am–5pm daily

Wat Prayun
An artificial hill covered with *chedi* (stupas) and temples is the highlight at Wat Prayun. Devotees release turtles in the pond nearby.
🕲 Pratchatipok Road • Map C6
• Open 8am–6pm daily

Church of Santa Cruz
This church was built by the Portuguese in 1782. The present building, with its pastel colors and octagonal dome, dates back to 1913. 🕲 Soi Kudi Chin • Map C6
• Open 5–8pm Mon–Sat, 9am–8pm Sun

Wat Suwannaram
This temple is home to superb murals from the *Jataka Tales*, which tell the story of the Buddha's previous lives. 🕲 33 Charan Sanit Wong Soi 32 • Map S5
• (02) 433 8045 • Open 6am–5pm daily

Prasart Museum
Set in a landscaped garden, this museum features artworks housed in reproductions of famous buildings. 🕲 9 Krungthep Kreetha Soi 4A • Map U6 • (02) 379 3607 • Open 10am–3pm Thu–Sun by appointment • Adm

Bangkok Dolls Museum
This museum displays dolls from around the world, all dressed in miniature costumes and set in context (see p46).

Price Categories

For a meal for one made up of one or two dishes served with a soft drink and including service.

B	under B100
BB	B100–200
BBB	B200–500
BBBB	B500–1,000
BBBBB	over B1,000

Above **Baan Khanitha**

TOP 10 Restaurants

Maha Naga
The intriguing mix of fusion and traditional Thai dishes makes guests want to linger at Maha Naga. ◈ *2 Sukhumvit Soi 29 • Map T6 • (02) 662 3060 • Open 5:30pm–11pm daily • www.mahanaga.com • BBBB*

Blue Elephant
Housed in a stunning century-old building, the Blue Elephant specializes in Royal Thai Cuisine, with dishes such as "Blue Elephant Classics." ◈ *233 South Sathorn Road • Map N6 • (02) 673 9353–8 • Open 11:30am–2:30pm & 6:30–10:30pm daily • www.blueelephant.com • BBBBB*

Baan Khanitha
One of the city's longest-running upscale restaurants, this place serves classic Thai dishes. ◈ *69 South Sathorn Road • Map T6 • (02) 675 4200–1 • Open 11am–11pm daily • www.baan-khanitha.com • BBBB*

Le Lys
This restaurant serves traditional Thai dishes without making them too spicy to suit the Western palate. ◈ *148/11 Nang Linchi Soi 6 • Map T6 • (02) 287 1898 • Open 11am–10pm daily • www.lelys. info • BBB*

Cabbages & Condoms
A good range of Thai dishes at a reasonable price makes this restaurant a good choice, especially as proceeds go toward AIDS prevention programs. ◈ *6–8 Sukhumvit Soi 12 • Map T6 • (02) 229 4610 • Open 11am–10pm daily • BBBB*

Le Dalat
Bangkok's premier Vietnamese restaurant serves a host of exquisitely prepared traditional dishes. ◈ *57 Soi Prasanmitr, Sukhumvit 23 • Map T6 • (02) 259 9593 • 11:30am–2:30pm & 5:30–10:30pm daily • BBB*

Indus
With a menu of Indian and Thai dishes, Indus serves both meat and vegetarian options. ◈ *7 Sukhumvit Soi 26 • Map T6 • (02) 258 4900 • Open 11am–2:30pm & 6–11pm daily • BBBB*

Supatra River House
The riverside views are a great attraction at Supatra River House, and the seafood is also excellent. ◈ *266 Soi Wat Rakhang • Map A4 • (02) 411 0305 • Open 11:30am–2:30pm & 5:30–11pm daily • BBBBB*

Celadon
This award-winning restaurant serves sublime Thai food. The surrounding lotus pond provides the perfect setting. ◈ *Sukhothai Hotel, 13/3 South Sathorn Road • Map Q5 • (02) 344 8888 • Open noon–3pm & 6:30–11pm daily • BBBBB*

Basil
Savor delicious Thai dishes such as snow fish curry in sophisticated surroundings. ◈ *Sheraton Grande Sukhumvit, 250 Sukhumvit Road • Map T6 • (02) 649 8366 • Open noon–2:30pm & 6–10:30pm daily • BBBBB*

Left **Bull's Head** Center **Cheap Charlie's** Right **The Londoner Brew Pub**

⑩ Bars and Pubs

Bacchus
A welcoming venue with a variety of lounge and dance areas on its four floors, which attracts a good crowd. ✆ *20/6–7 Soi Ruam Rudi • Map T6 • (02) 650 8986 • Open 4pm–1am daily*

Bull's Head
Judging by the regulars who drop by for the happy hour, the quiz nights, and the pub grub, the Bull's Head has made a success of recreating the atmosphere of an English pub. ✆ *Sukhumvit Soi 33/1 • Map T6 • (02) 259 4444 • Open 11am–1am daily*

Jools Bar
For anyone curious about the go-go bars of Nana Plaza but not quite ready to step inside, this place offers a convenient spot from which to view the action, with reasonably priced beers. ✆ *21/3 Sukhumvit Soi 4 • Map T6 • (02) 252 6413 • Open 9am–1am daily*

Nest at Le Fenix Hotel
Sofas and rattan beds are dotted about this bar set in stylish rooftop gardens. A retractable roof comes in handy during rainstorms. ✆ *33 Sukhumvit Soi 11 • Map T6 • (02) 255 0638–9 • Open 6pm–2am daily*

Zanzibar
This Italian restaurant/jazz bar/karaoke lounge has been a hit since day one, with jazz in the early evening and dancing later on. ✆ *139 Sukhumvit Soi 11 • Map T6 • (02) 651 2700 • Open 5pm–2am daily*

Long Table
There are amazing views over Bangkok at this restaurant/bar. The happy hour is from 5 until 7pm. ✆ *25th floor, 48 Column Tower, Sukhumvit Road, Soi 16 • Map T6 • (02) 302 2557 • Open 5pm–2am daily*

Tuba
A second-hand furniture shop and restaurant by day; by night a place to play pool and listen to some 70s tunes. ✆ *30 Soi 21, Sukhumvit Road, Soi 63 • Map T6 • (02) 711 5500 • Open 11am–2am daily*

Black Swan
As the name suggests, this is a British-style pub offering a wide range of imported beers and generous portions of typical pub food. ✆ *326/8–9 Sukhumvit Road • Map T6 • (02) 626 0257 • Open 8am–1am daily*

The Londoner Brew Pub
With pretty barmaids, its own brew of beer, long happy hours, and free Wi-Fi access, this cavernous bar goes that extra step to keep its customers happy. ✆ *Basement UBC II Building, Sukhumvit Soi 33 • Map T6 • (02) 261 0238–9 • Open 11am–1am daily*

Cheap Charlie's
It's nothing but a stall with a few bar stools on a side street, yet the cheap beers and friendly vibe make Cheap Charlie's something of a Bangkok institution. ✆ *Sukhumvit Soi 11 • Map T6 • Open 3pm–1am daily*

Left **Saxophone** Center **Calypso Cabaret** Right **Q Bar**

🔟 Nightclubs and Entertainment

1 Adhere the 13th
This club may be small, but the combination of a band, cheap beer, and friendly vibe make it a popular hangout (see p42).

2 Saxophone
Moderate prices and impressive music bring a mixed crowd of Thais and foreigners to Saxophone (see p42).

3 Bed Supperclub
Looking like a spaceship that has just landed, this super-hip club is hugely popular despite the pricey drinks and set-menu meals. Some nights are themed, so check out the website before getting dressed up (see p42).

4 Q Bar
One of Bangkok's most fashionable nightspots, this club occupies two floors and a terrace, with a dance floor that gets plenty of use. It often hosts top international DJs (see p42).

5 Witch's Tavern
Housed in a Victorian-style building, Witch's Tavern serves great burgers and unique cocktails. The house band plays mostly covers of favorite rock ballads as requested by the audience (see p43).

6 Tawandang German Brewery
You can get a big helping of home-brewed beer accompanied by big bands playing *morlam*

music from northeast Thailand at this huge party palace. ✆ 462/61 Narathiwat Ratchanakharin • Map U4 • (02) 678 1114–5 • Open 5pm–1am daily

7 Titanium Bar
Cool, sleek and refined, but also fun and unpretentious, Titanium plays host to "the best all-girl rock band in Thailand". They play mostly covers, but really know how to make it swing. ✆ Sukhumvit Soi 22 • Map T6 • (02) 258 3758 • Open 8pm–2am daily

8 Living Room
A stylish hang-out, Living Room features top-class jazz musicians every evening. It has a sophisticated ambience in which to enjoy a cocktail and chat, or just soak up the sounds. ✆ Sheraton Grande Hotel • Map T6 • (02) 649 8888 • Open 9pm–midnight daily

9 Calypso Cabaret
Only in Thailand could you find such a show: transvestites looking sensational in sequins and stockings, lip-synching and dancing to pop songs, with well-choreographed dance routines (see p45).

10 Siam Niramit
One of the largest stage productions in the world, featuring over 150 performers, 500 costumes, and lots of special effects that take the audience on a spectacular journey to the enchanted kingdom of Thailand (see p44).

Left **Croc-wrestling show at Crocodile Farm** Right **Bridge on the Kwai River**

Beyond Bangkok

BANGKOK'S SIGHTS ARE LIABLE TO *cause sensory overload, from the dazzling temples to the constant crowds. Fortunately, when visitors feel that they need a break there are plenty of opportunities for a day trip or an overnight stay away from the city. Tour operators can arrange undemanding and entertaining trips to nearby attractions, such as the Floating Market, the Rose Garden, the Ancient City, and the Crocodile Farm. For an excursion with more cultural content, head for the ruins of Ayutthaya, the country's ancient capital, or Kanchanaburi, where the bridge over the Kwai River and the Allied Cemetery mark a tragic phase of World War II. If it is tropical beaches you long for, make for Pattaya, or Koh Samed with its powder-soft sands.*

Nakhon Pathom Chedi

Thai temple, Bang Pa-In

🔟 Sights

1. Muang Boran (Ancient City)
2. Crocodile Farm
3. Rose Garden
4. Damnoen Saduak Floating Market
5. Nakhon Pathom Chedi
6. Ayutthaya
7. Bang Pa-In
8. Kanchanaburi
9. Pattaya
10. Koh Samed

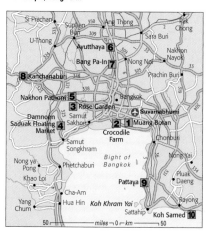

Prince of Lampang's Palace, Muang Boran

Muang Boran (Ancient City)
Covering a huge 320 acres (130 hectares) designed in the shape of Thailand, this cultural park contains reconstructions of some of the country's most famous temples and monuments. It may sound like a tacky theme park, but the site offers a visually impressive and informative experience. Visitors can explore the site by car, tram, or bicycle, and it is rarely crowded.

20 miles (33 km) from Bangkok on Sukhumvit Road, Bangpoo • Map T2 • (02) 709 1644 • Open 8am–5pm daily • Adm • www.ancientcity.com

Crocodile Farm
With over 60,000 freshwater and saltwater crocodiles, this is the world's largest crocodile farm. It has the biggest crocodile ever kept in captivity – a 20-ft (6-m) monster weighing over 2,200 lb (1,000 kg). The highlight of the farm is the hourly show, in which handlers wrestle with crocodiles and even put their heads in the creatures' mouths. The farm also has a zoo, an amusement park, and a souvenir shop that sells goods made from crocodile skin.

1 mile (2 km) E of Samut Prakan • Map T2 • (02) 703 5144–8 • Open 7am–6pm (shows hourly, 9am–4pm) daily • Adm

Rose Garden
Located just a short ride from downtown Bangkok, this resort features several attractions in its 70 acres (28 hectares) of grounds. These include botanical gardens with many types of roses and orchids, a cultural village, restaurants, a golf course, a spa, and a large hotel. A daily cultural show features dances from different regions of the country, as well as a Thai boxing bout, sword fighting, and a Thai wedding ceremony. Visitors also have the option of an elephant ride.

20 miles (32 km) from Bangkok on Pet Kasem Road, Sampran • Map T2 • (034) 322 544 • Open 8am–6pm daily; cultural show 2:45pm • Adm

Damnoen Saduak Floating Market
Although this floating market is considered by some to be nothing more than a show put on for tourists, it is certainly the best example of its kind. The market gives an idea of how life in this region once revolved around small boats plying their trade on narrow canals. Arrive early (or even better, stay overnight) to avoid the crowds emerging from tour buses at around 10am, and you will be rewarded with images of smiling Thais in traditional clothes, *sampan* (flat-bottomed boats) piled high with appetizing fruits, and bowls of noodles served directly from floating kitchens *(see pp20–21)*.

Damnoen Saduak Floating Market

The Death Railway

Between 1942 and 1945, an estimated 16,000 Allied prisoners-of-war and around 100,000 Asians lost their lives during the construction of a railroad line from Thailand to Burma. The Japanese saw the line as crucial to their occupation of Southeast Asia, so after the Japanese surrender, the British tore up the track and the rail link was never re-established.

Nakhon Pathom Chedi

At 395 ft (120 m), this *chedi* (stupa) is one of the world's tallest Buddhist monuments. Dating back to at least the 6th century, it attained its current magnificent proportions during the reign of Rama V (r.1868–1910). An important pilgrimage site, it is often busy with Thais making offerings at various altars. The *chedi* is surrounded by four *wihan* (assembly halls) at the cardinal points, and niches in the cloisters contain Buddha images in unusual *mudra* (postures). ◈ *35 miles (56 km) W of Bangkok • Map T2 • (034) 242 143 • Open 6am–6pm daily • Adm*

Ayutthaya

From 1350 to 1767, Ayutthaya ruled supreme as the capital of its own kingdom, only to be abandoned after being sacked by the Burmese *(see pp34)*. The Ayutthaya Historical Park is a must-see for anyone interested in Thailand's rich history, with its ancient ruins set in tranquil countryside. The most important temples – Wat Mahathat, Wat Ratchaburuna, and Wat Sri Sanphet – are centrally located and can be covered in a day trip *(see pp28–31)*.

Bang Pa-In

While visiting Ayutthaya, it is well worth stopping off at the nearby royal retreat of Bang Pa-In. Established by King Prasat Thong (r.1629–56) in the mid-17th century and expanded by Rama IV and Rama V *(see p34)*, its exuberant buildings are an eclectic mix of Thai architecture, particularly in the Aisawan Thipphaya-at pavilion, and European influences, as seen in the Phra Thinang Warophat Phiman. The manicured lawns and tranquil lakes give the place a relaxed feel *(see p30)*.

Kanchanaburi

At the western edge of the Central Plains, Kanchanaburi is a popular day trip from Bangkok. The main sights are the bridge over the Kwai River and the war cemeteries where thousands of allied soldiers who died in World War II during the construction of the "Death Railway" to Burma are buried. The Thailand-Burma Railway Center does a good job of explaining the context in which the disastrous events unfolded. On a lighter note, Kanchanaburi is also the jumping-off point for several beautiful natural sites, including the Erawan National Park with its refreshing waterfalls. ◈ *80 miles (130 km) W of Bangkok • Map S2*

Wat Mahathat, Ayutthaya

9 Pattaya

Pattaya is infamous for its go-go bars, discos, and transvestite cabarets as well as countless "bar beers" – open-sided bars with friendly hostesses. Yet the town has made an attempt to clean up its image, and there are now some family attractions, such as Pattaya Park Water Park, Underwater World, Mini Siam, and an Elephant Village. Watersports and golf are also big here, and there is plenty of choice for eating and shopping, with some excellent seafood restaurants and well-stocked shopping malls. ✆ 91 miles (147 km) SE of Bangkok • Map U3

Pattaya bars and restaurants

10 Koh Samed

Just 31 miles (50 km) east of Pattaya, Koh Samed is easily the best beach escape from the capital. As it is an island, the waters around it are much clearer, and the quality of the sand much finer than anything to be found on the mainland. Unfortunately, due to its popularity, accommodation rates have spiralled, despite it being a national park. By avoiding weekends and public holidays, it is possible to enjoy the idyllic surroundings without feeling like a sardine in a can. ✆ 124 miles (200 km) SE of Bangkok • Map U3

A Day and a Night in Pattaya

Morning

Start the day relaxing on **Jomtien Beach** (see p52), a seemingly endless stretch of sand just south of Pattaya town center. Take a swim to cool down or if you are feeling energetic have a go at windsurfing, parasailing, or water-skiing. If you haven't been snacking all morning on seafood or fruit sold by wandering vendors on the beach, head for **Bruno's** near the north end of the beach for a sumptuous steak or lobster lunch.

Afternoon

After lunch, head up to **Khao Phra Tamnak** from where there are excellent views of Pattaya Beach. Next, head north of town to the **Sanctuary of Truth**, a fabulous palace that blends influences from Khmer, Hindu, and Buddhist architecture. Finish the afternoon's sightseeing with a visit to **Mini Siam**, which features miniature models of some of the country's most famous buildings.

Night

After a rest and shower in the hotel, head out for a taste of Pattaya's nightlife. Begin in any of the beachfront bar beers, where you can get a feel for the party mood of the town. For dinner, go to **PIC Kitchen** in Soi 5 and indulge in a delicious curry or freshly grilled seafood. Next, check out a Thai transvestite cabaret at **Tiffany's**. After the show, decide whether to head for bed or make a deeper exploration of Pattaya's pulsating nightlife.

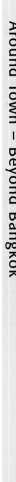

Around Town – Beyond Bangkok

STREETSMART

BANGKOK'S TOP 10

Left **Thai coins** Right **Duty-free shopping, Suvarnabhumi Airport**

ⓉOP10 Planning Your Trip

1 Passports and Visas

All visitors to Thailand must be in possession of a passport valid for at least six months from the date of entry. Travelers from most Western countries are given a tourist visa on arrival that is valid for 30 days. For longer visits, it is better to apply for a 60-day visa from the Thai embassy in your home country. The visa must be used within three months of being issued. Non-immigrant visas lasting 90 days are also available if there is a good reason for an extended stay, such as education or business. A 60-day visa can be extended for 30 days, or a 30-day visa for 10 days, by applying to the Immigration Office (see p109) and paying a fee. If you overstay your visa, there is a B500 fine per day. Since these visa regulations are subject to change, it is best to check the Thai Ministry of Foreign Affairs website.

2 When to Go

The best time to visit Bangkok is between November and February, when clear skies are guaranteed and temperatures are a bit cooler than the rest of the year, generally below 80°F (26.5°C). However, hotel rates are generally higher and tourist attractions more crowded. The hot season from March to May is fine for a

beach holiday but not so good for strenuous activities. The rainy season – between June and October – can be pleasant, and storms usually blow over quickly.

3 What to Take

Light, loose-fitting clothes are ideal for Bangkok throughout the year. Long-sleeved shirts, a hat, and sunscreen are necessary for protection from the sun, and an umbrella is invaluable during the rains. Warm clothing is only needed in the hills of northern Thailand.

4 Health Considerations

Inoculations are not compulsory in Thailand, and pharmacies in Bangkok are generally very well stocked, so only special medications need to be carried. Health or travel insurance with good cover is a must.

5 Customs

The duty-free allowance for all passengers arriving in Thailand is 200 cigarettes or nine ounces (250 g) of tobacco and a liter of wines or spirits.

6 Time Differences

Thailand is seven hours ahead of Greenwich Mean Time, 12 hours ahead of US Eastern Standard Time, and three hours behind Australian Eastern Standard Time.

7 Currency

Thailand's currency is the baht (B), which is divided into 100 satang. Coins come in denominations of B1, B2, B5, and B10. 25- and 50-satang coins are rarely seen. Notes are available for B20 (green), B50 (blue), B100 (red), B500 (purple), and B1,000 (brown).

8 Language

Being a tonal language, Thai is not easy for Westerners, though learning a few key phrases (see pp126–8) will make you popular with locals. Fortunately, English is widely spoken in most tourist areas.

9 Driving

Driving yourself around Bangkok is not recommended. Those keen to rent a car will need an international driver's license, though many rental companies will accept a valid national license.

10 Electricity

The electric current in Thailand is 220 volts AC, 50 cycles, and most plug sockets are of the two-pin variety. Adaptors are readily available in department stores.

Passports & Visas

Thai Ministry of Foreign Affairs:
www.mfa.go.th

 Preceding pages **Fruit vendor at Damnoen Saduak Floating Market**

Left **Suvarnabhumi Airport, Bangkok** Right **Traffic snarls**

TOP 10 Arriving in Bangkok

1 By Air
The majority of travelers to Bangkok arrive by air, and its airport is served by over 80 airlines with direct flights from some of the world's major cities. Thai Airways has an extensive network and budget airlines, such as Air Asia, operate flights within Thailand and to several destinations in Southeast Asia.

2 Flight Bookings
Booking well in advance can make big savings and is a necessity during the peak season between November and February, when all flights can be full. By booking online, you can check rates of various airlines and get the best deal.

3 Suvarnabhumi Airport
Suvarnabhumi International Airport has the world's biggest terminal. International and domestic flights all operate from the same terminal, with arrivals on level 2 and departures on level 4. The airport is located around 16 miles (25 km) east of Bangkok.

4 Airport Services
As might be expected from such a super-modern facility, Suvarnabhumi is well equipped to cater for travelers, with plenty of shops, restaurants, lounges, and day rooms for passengers needing a rest during a long layover. Information counters operated by Airports of Thailand (AOT) are at the exit from levels 2 and 4.

5 From the Airport: by Taxi
Metered public taxis, with a "Taximeter" sign on the roof, are both convenient and affordable. The taxi assignment desks are on level 2 outside doors 4 and 9. A journey to downtown Bangkok costs about B300–400, including a B50 airport surcharge. The much-touted airport limousine service is far more expensive.

6 From the Airport: by Train
The high-speed, non-stop Suvarnabhumi Airport Rail Link (SARL) takes only 15 minutes to reach the City Air Terminal at Makkasan station, or 18 minutes to central Phaya Thai station. It is by far the quickest form of transport into town.

7 Don Muang Airport
Bangkok's old international airport, located 16 miles (25 km) north of Bangkok, serves as a hub for domestic and international low cost airlines. These include Nok Air, Nok Mini, Air Asia, and Orient Thai Airlines. Flights serve every corner of Thailand including Chiang Mai, Phuket, and Koh Samui.

8 Car Rental
Several international and local companies offer car hire from the transportation center near the airport.

9 Arriving by Bus
With its well-developed transport system, Thailand fits well into overland itineraries that include visits to neighboring countries. Buses from Malaysia terminate at the Southern Bus Terminal, while those from Cambodia and Laos pull up at the Northern Bus Terminal.

10 Arriving by Train
It is possible to reach Bangkok from Singapore and Malaysia by train. All trains terminate at the Hua Lampong Station.

Transport Links

Hua Lampong Station:
Rama IV Road; Map F6 ; (02) 225 6964; Subway Hua Lampong

Northern Bus Terminal: *Phahonyothin Road; Map T5; (02) 272 0299; Skytrain Mo Chit*

Southern Bus Terminal: *Borommarat Chonnani Road; Map S5; (02) 435 1199; AC bus 507, 511*

Suvarnabhumi Airport: *www. airportsuvarnabhumi. com*

Left **A busy Bangkok road** Center **BTS Skytrain** Right *Tuk-tuk*

Getting Around Bangkok

1 BTS Skytrain
The BTS Skytrain is the most speedy and efficient way of getting around. There are two lines – the Sukhumvit line, which runs from Mo Chit to Bearing along Sukhumvit Road, and the Silom line, from the National Stadium to Bang Wa. The lines intersect at Siam Square. If you plan to make several journeys, buy a One-Day Pass for B130 (unlimited trips) or a Rabbit Card (smart card) for B200 whose stored value lasts for 2 years. The Skytrain connects to a high-speed rail link to Suvarnabhumi Airport at Phaya Thai station. ◎ *(02) 617 7340–2 • 6am–midnight • www.bts.co.th*

2 MRT Subway
Bangkok's MRT subway system covers a loop of 12 miles (20 km) from Hua Lampong Station to Bang Sue north of the center. It intersects with the Skytrain at four stations, and fares cost B16–40. ◎ *(02) 354 2000 • 6am–midnight • www.bangkokmetro.co.th*

3 Bus
Bangkok has an extensive bus network with very cheap fares. Most routes operate from 4am to 10pm, while a few provide a 24-hour service. They can get stuck in heavy traffic, so an air-conditioned bus is a good option. ◎ *(02) 246 0973 • www.bmta.co.th*

4 Boat
The Chao Phraya River and the few remaining canals provide commuter-style transport, a faster option to the horrendous traffic on Bangkok's roads. A good way to get to Old City sights is on the Chao Phraya Express boat. There are several river ferries and also commuter boats that ply the canals. ◎ *Chao Phraya Express boats • (02) 445 8888 • www.chaophraya expressboat.com*

5 Taxi
Metered taxis are easy to find and relatively cheap, with a flag fare of B35 for the first 1.5 miles (2 km) and B5 for every 0.6 mile (1 km) after that. Insist on using the meter as it is cheaper than negotiating a fare.

6 Tuk-Tuk
For many visitors, a ride in a *tuk-tuk* is an essential part of the Thai experience, and it can be exciting weaving through the traffic in these open-sided three-wheelers. However, they are noisy and unprotected from pollution. Fares need to be negotiated before you start *(see p109)*.

7 Motorbike Taxi
Motorbike taxi riders in numbered vests who wait on the corners of important side roads are useful for routes not covered by other modes of transport. Fares are negotiable. While they are fast and can squeeze through traffic jams they can be dangerous – so hang on tight.

8 On Foot
Given the problems with Bangkok's traffic, it is best to visit just one area in a day, and explore it on foot. This is a particularly good way to reach the sights in the Old City and Chinatown, and also for the shopping districts of Siam Square and Silom Road.

9 Guided Tours
Planning a journey in a crowded, unfamiliar city can be difficult, so many people opt for a guided tour. While such tours may be enjoyable and informative, they are also expensive and preclude encounters with local people that can lead to stimulating cultural exchanges.

10 Maps
For independent exploration of Bangkok, the latest Skytrain and Subway route maps are essential; most hotels and guesthouses should have one. For buses, use *Bus Routes & Map*, readily available in most bookshops. Shoppers might like to buy Nancy Chandler's *Map of Bangkok*, full of colorful, hand-drawn maps with detailed notes about shops and markets throughout the city.

Left **A Thai man reading a newspaper** Center **Stairs to the Golden Mount** Right **Pantip Plaza**

⓾ Bangkok on a Budget

1 Sleeping
Most budget travelers head for Khao San Road on the northern fringe of the Old City for rooms that cost less than B325 a night. Though it still offers the best range of budget accommodations (see p117), the area is gradually going upscale. Chinatown and Downtown also have a few cheap options.

2 Eating
Unless you dine in fancy restaurants, eating is not expensive in Bangkok. Costs can be kept to a minimum by eating at food stalls on street corners. Some of the best stalls specialize in one dish such as phat thai, which will fill you up for around B40–50. Food courts in malls also serve a tasty and cheap lunch.

3 Drinking
Save money on your alcohol bill by sticking to local beers (Chang, Leo, Singha) and spirits (Mekhong and Sang Som), which are much cheaper than imports. Look out for Happy Hours and two-for-one deals.

4 Free Magazines and Events
There are several free magazines for tourists, such as BK Magazine, which give reviews of new restaurants and bars, and listings of events in the city. They are distributed through hotels and tourist offices.

5 SIM Cards
If you want to use your mobile phone while in Bangkok but avoid expensive international roaming rates, go to a mobile phone shop and buy a SIM card for a few dollars. This will provide you with a new number that will enable you to call at local rates, and the deal often includes a number of free calls.

6 Parks
Taking a stroll in a park is an enjoyable way to relax, get some exercise, and see how the Thais make the most of their leisure time. Near the center of Bangkok is Lumphini Park (see p80), which is large, but can get crowded in the mornings and evenings. For a more laid-back experience, visit the Rama IX Royal Park (see p90), which has lots of paths and well-landscaped gardens.

7 Temples
Apart from the main temples, such as Wat Phra Kaeo (see pp8–11) and Wat Pho (see pp14–15), there is no entrance fee to temple compounds in Thailand. These compounds are often a treasure trove of art and architecture, and resident monks are often keen to learn about their visitors from afar, so going to a temple can be a great way to learn about Thai culture and customs.

8 Traditional Massage
If you fancy pampering your body at a spa without the expensive price tag, and provided you can live without the luxurious surroundings and little extras like herbal teas and ambient music, then settle for a traditional Thai massage. A two-hour session should not cost more than B500, and will probably leave you feeling that you are floating on air.

9 River Bus
To explore life on the Chao Phraya River without joining a guided tour, take the Chao Phraya Express from any pier heading north to Nonthaburi, and watch locals going about their business on boats and along the banks of the river. The round trip takes a couple of hours and costs less than B65.

10 Window Shopping
Unless you are a compulsive buyer, countless hours of fun can be had window shopping, which is something of a national pastime for the Thais. The shopping malls around Siam Square and Ratchadamri Road are ideal for this activity, offering air-conditioned comfort, cheap food courts, and entertainment in the form of cinemas, bowling, and ice skating.

Left **ATM booth** Center **Public phone booth** Right **Thai stamps**

Banking and Communications

1 Banks
Most banks are open between 8:30am and 3:30pm but branches in airports or department stores often stay open later. Big branches have a foreign exchange counter and can arrange inter-national transfers.
Ⓢ Bangkok Bank: 333 Silom Road • Map P5 • (02) 645 5555 • www.bangkokbank.com Ⓢ Thai Military Bank: 3000 Phaholyothin Road • Map N3 • (02) 299 1111 • www.tmbbank.com

2 ATM Services
ATM machines are easy to find in Bangkok. There are usually one or more units outside each bank branch, and they can also be found at gas stations and department stores. All offer an English language option and accept major credit and debit cards, but a service charge is applied.

3 Changing Money
The baht exchange rate fluctuates daily but the best rate is offered by banks. There is little need to bring traveler's checks.

4 Credit Cards
VISA and MasterCard credit and debit cards are accepted by all major banks, department stores (which can apply a hefty charge), travel agents, hotels, and many restaurants. Diners Club and American Express are not widely accepted.

5 Post
Post office hours are normally 8:30am–4:30pm from Monday to Friday and 9am–noon on Saturday. Letters to or from Europe or the US usually take a week or more to arrive. For important documents use the Express Mail Service (EMS) or register the letter for an extra fee.

6 Telephones
There are several types of public phone: some coin- or card-operated, some local or international. Phone cards are generally sold in convenience stores. For regular calls, it is easier to rent a mobile phone or buy a SIM card. Charges for making calls from your hotel can be steep.

7 Calling to and from Bangkok
The country code for Thailand is 66 and the code for Bangkok is 02. When making calls within Bangkok, dial 02 before the seven-digit number. To call abroad, dial the international access code 001, then country code. When phoning the UK, US, and much of Europe, the alternative prefix 008 offers a reduced rate and the code 009 accesses Voice-Over-Internet Protocol (VOIP). It is cheaper to call at night – rates are reduced by 20–30 percent between 9pm and 7am.

8 Internet Access
Broadband is now ubiquitous in Thailand so downloading information is usually very fast. There are Internet cafés all over the city, particularly in tourist and shopping areas like Khao San Road, Siam Square, and Silom Road, with rates averaging about a baht a minute. Many guesthouses and hotels offer Internet access, sometimes free to guests. Wi-Fi is becoming increasingly available in many locations including hotels, cafés, bars, guesthouses, and some shops.

9 Newspapers
There are two English dailies – Bangkok Post and The Nation; both carry a mix of local and international news, as well as features and listings of events in daily supplements. Same-day issues of national newspapers from other countries, such as the Sun from the UK and USA Today are sold in some bookshops, though prices for these are steep.

10 Television and Radio
Watching Thai TV can be interesting, but the Thai language can be a barrier for foreigners. Many hotels, and a few guest-houses, offer satellite TV. There are also a few radio stations that broadcast in English, such as Eazy FM and Radio Thailand.

Streetsmart

ขายยา

Left **A rattan fan** Center **Pharmacy signboard** Right **Tourist Police patrol car**

🔟 Security and Health

1 Emergency Numbers

In an emergency, or if you are the victim of a crime, call the Tourist Police. When reporting a crime, you will need to file a report at a police station. If you are ill or injured, call the Emergency Medical Institute Hotline. To report dishonest dealings by tour operators or shopkeepers, contact the Tourist Service Center.

2 Personal Security

Although Bangkok is relatively safe, it is wise to keep cash in a money belt and avoid wearing expensive jewelry. Watch out for pickpockets in crowded areas, such as Chatuchak Weekend Market (see pp22–3).

3 Scams

Unfortunately, some Thais exploit their country's reputation for hospitality to fleece tourists. Common scams involve *tuk-tuk* drivers, gem dealers, and independent tour guides. Con-artists are inventive, so avoid getting drawn into conversation with unnaturally friendly Thais.

4 Embassies

If you happen to lose your passport or get into trouble with the police, contact your embassy. They can issue replacement passports or offer legal assistance if necessary. ◈ UK Embassy: 14 Wireless Road • Map R3

• (02) 305 8333
• www.gov.uk/government/world/thailand
◈ US Embassy: 120/22 Wireless Road • Map R4 (02) 205 4000 • http://bangkok.usembassy.gov

5 Hospitals and Clinics

Thai hospitals are hygienic, efficient, and inexpensive, with a high ratio of doctors to patients. The Bumrungrad Hospital and Bangkok Nursing Home Hospital have high standards of health care. For minor ailments, local clinics are also reliable, and most staff speak essential English. ◈ Bumrungrad Hospital: Sukhumvit Soi 3 • Map T5 • (02) 667 1000 ◈ BNH Hospital: 9 convent Road • Map P5
• (02) 686 2700

6 Pharmacies

Pharmacies are generally well-stocked with medicines, including antibiotics, for which prescriptions are not necessary. Opening times are usually 9am–6pm, though in tourist areas like Silom and Sukhumvit, some places stay open until midnight.

7 Dentists

As with general medical healthcare, dental treatment is comparatively much cheaper than in the West. In fact this itself can be reason enough for a trip. Most dentists speak some English and are generally competent.

◈ Dental Hospital: 88/88 Sukhumvit Soi 49 • Map T6 • (02) 260 5000–15

8 Heat and Humidity

For temperate zone visitors, the heat and humidity can be a shock to the system. Avoid walking in the midday sun, wear a hat, use plenty of sunscreen, and carry a fan. Drink plenty of water to avoid dehydration.

9 Water

Though tap water in Bangkok is generally safe to drink, bottled water is safer still; it is also cheap and widely available. There is no problem with ice in restaurants, but it is best to avoid drinks with crushed ice that are sold at roadside stalls.

10 Air Pollution

The combination of dust and exhaust fumes on the streets of Bangkok causes air pollution that can reach dangerous levels. If you are sensitive to such conditions, buy a face mask, and avoid open road transport.

Emergencies

Medical Hotline:
1669

Tourist Service Center:
1155

Tourist Police:
1155
• www.thailand touristpolice.com

Left **Colorful Tourist Authority of Thailand brochures** Right **Asia Books**

🔟 Useful Information

1 Tourist Information

The Tourist Authority of Thailand (TAT), the official government tourist board, has offices worldwide and its headquarters in Bangkok. Its website provides comprehensive coverage of destinations and events, and maps and brochures are available from its office. The Bangkok Tourist Bureau (BTB) is also a useful source of information and has booths in many of the city's tourist areas.
⊗ *Tourist Authority of Thailand: 1600 Phetburi Tat Mai Road • Map T5 • (02) 250 5500 • www.tourismthailand.org* ⊗ *Bangkok Tourist Bureau: 17/1 Phra Athit Road • Map B2 • (02) 225 7612–4 • www.bangkoktourist.com*

2 Opening Hours

Most government offices are open from 8:30am to 4:30pm, but many close for lunch between noon and 1pm. Tourist attractions tend to stay open from 9am to 5pm, with last tickets being sold until an hour prior to closing. Department stores generally open at 10am and close at 9pm or 10pm. On public holidays government offices, banks, and post offices are closed but most shops remain open.

3 Public Holidays

New Year's Day (Jan 1), Makha Bucha (Feb/ Mar), Chakri Day (Apr 6), Songkran (Apr 13–15), Labor Day (May 1), Coronation Day (May 5), Visakha Bucha (May/Jun), Khao Phansa (Jul), Queen's Birthday (Aug 12), Chulalongkorn Day (Oct 23), King's Birthday (Dec 5), Constitution Day (Dec 10).

4 Disabled Travelers

Unfortunately there is little provision for disabled travelers in Bangkok, with only a few top-end hotels offering wheelchair ramps and other facilities. The city streets, which are a headache for all pedestrians with their uneven pavements and potholes, are nothing short of a nightmare for disabled visitors.

5 Gay and Lesbian Travelers

The tolerant attitude to homosexuality, both male and female, makes Bangkok an attractive destination for gay and lesbian travelers. There are a lot of bars where the clientele is mostly gay *(see p43)*. However, public displays of affection are usually frowned upon.

6 Drinking Age

You must be 18 years or over to buy alcohol in Thailand. Most nightclubs refuse entry to anyone under 20. The rules are strictly enforced, so do not forget to carry your passport or ID card.

7 Websites

For reviews of hotels and restaurants, plus information about Thai culture and festivals, visit www.bangkok.com. For information concerning visas and work permits go to www.thaivisa.com.

8 Event Listings

Upcoming events are publicized in newspapers, *BK Magazine*, and on www.bk.asia-city.com/events. For tickets to sporting events and music concerts, log on to www.thaiticketmajor.com.

9 Bookshops

It is easy to find books in English but the selection is often limited. Asia Books, Bookazine, and Kinokuniya have a wide range of books. Sections 1 and 27 of Chatuchak Weekend Market *(see pp22–3)* have a fascinating mix of old magazines and discounted art books.
⊗ *Asia Books: (02) 715 9000 • www.asiabooks.com* ⊗ *Bookazine: (02) 231 0016 • www.bookazine.co.th* ⊗ *Kinokuniya: (02) 610 9500 • www.kinokuniya.com*

10 Buddhist Era

Thailand uses the Western calendar for banking and business purposes, but it follows the Buddhist Era (BE) for everything else. This is measured from Buddha's Enlightenment, which was in 543 BC. Thus AD 2014 is 2557 BE in Thailand.

Left **Sign at Wat Phra Kaeo** Right **Bars and pubs along a busy street**

TOP 10 Things to Avoid

1 Showing Disrespect to the Royal Family
Thais are devoted to the royal family and show utmost respect to the king, the queen, and their children. While they are generally tolerant of foreigners breaking cultural taboos, no such leniency is shown for disrespecting the monarchy. This includes acts that might seem inconsequential in the West, such as not standing to attention when the national anthem is played in cinemas.

2 Wearing Disrespectful Dress to Temples
When visiting a temple in Thailand, do not wear shorts or sleeveless shirts. In the case of Wat Phra Kaeo, this also includes sandals. People who are inappropriately dressed need to rent clothes to cover the offending parts or they are refused entry.

3 Losing Your Temper
If you are dissatisfied with a Thai providing a service, the worst thing you can do is to raise your voice. Keep a "cool heart", or *jai yen* in Thai, and use charm to obtain your objective.

4 Illegal Drugs
Anyone caught in possession of, or trafficking in, illegal drugs is likely to face a long term in prison. Police make regular surprise raids on nightclubs, bars, and even guesthouses, conducting searches and taking random urine samples to identify drug users.

5 Taking a Tuk-Tuk Without Negotiating the Fare
If you travel anywhere by *tuk-tuk*, negotiate the fare before you start or you may end up paying much more than you bargained for. Unfortunately *tuk-tuk* drivers have a bad reputation for demanding an outrageous fee from passengers. To avoid this, ask someone in your guesthouse or hotel the approximate fare for the journey you plan to make.

6 Upstairs Bars on Patpong
While the go-go bars on Patpong are generally honest in their dealings, many upstairs bars advertise all kinds of sexual antics on stage but omit to state the prices or cover charge. After a couple of drinks, customers are presented with a bill for an extortionate amount and are not allowed to leave until they pay up. The simple solution is not to go upstairs.

7 Street Hustlers
In Bangkok's tourist areas a Thai might attempt to befriend you. Unfortunately, once in his confidence, he will offer to take you shopping for gems or souvenirs and pressure you into buying something, for which he will receive a commission. Be extremely wary of such "helpful" people.

8 Buying Gems
Selling fake or inferior quality gems to foreigners is one of the best-known and highly developed scams in Thailand, yet tourists continue to be cheated every day by the clever techniques used by hustlers. Unless you are an expert in identifying genuine gems, the best advice is not to be tempted by any mention of a good deal in gems.

9 Overstaying Your Visa
Visitors to Thailand often want to stay longer than initially planned. To do so simply go to the immigration office to extend your visa, or else you will have to pay a fine of B500 per day. § *Immigration Office: 507 Soi Suan Plu Sathorn • Map Q6 • (02) 287 3101–10 • www.immigration.go.th*

10 Unprotected Sex
Though Thailand has made impressive progress in AIDS awareness, the widespread prevalence of prostitution means that there is always the risk of contracting HIV if you practice unprotected sex. Condoms are cheap and widely available.

Left **Antiques on sale** Center **Chatuchak Weekend Market** Right **Siam Discovery Center**

🔟 Shopping Tips

1 Credit and Debit Cards

VISA and MasterCard are accepted in all major stores and boutiques, though several stores add on a surcharge which can be up to 5 percent of the purchase value. However, when shopping at street stalls and markets, all transactions must be in cash.

2 Shopping Malls and Department Stores

The massive and ultra-modern shopping malls in Siam Square, Silom, and Sukhumvit are like small cities, containing department stores, food courts, bowling alleys, designer boutiques, and skating rinks.

3 Markets and Street Stalls

Shopping in markets and at street stalls combines the opportunity to pick up bargains with cultural interaction. The best markets for textiles and ready-made clothes are Chatuchak, Phahurat, and Pratunam (see p38), while street stalls in Khao San Road, Patpong, and Sukhumvit Road are good for souvenirs.

4 Fake Goods

Thais have a knack of producing excellent copies of anything from branded watches to designer clothes and CDs at a fraction of the cost of the original. Such

breaches of copyright can result in occasional police raids that momentarily scare off vendors. As customs officials are entitled to seize fake goods, you just may return home empty-handed.

5 Bargaining

Prices are fixed in shopping malls and boutiques, but bargaining is expected in markets and at street stalls, where vendors quote a price that may be up to double the object's value. Begin by offering a figure less than what you are prepared to pay and gradually increase the offer until a deal is struck. If all else fails, walking away may persuade a vendor to drop the price.

6 Antiques

Thailand is the main outlet for antiques from across Southeast Asia. Unfortunately, many of the items available will have been stolen from temples in Burma and Cambodia. Occasionally, imitation antiques are passed off as the real thing. If you buy genuine antiques or Buddha images, you will need an export permit from the Fine Arts Department. The seller should help to arrange it but can take several days to process.

7 Crafts

Thai handicrafts make excellent gifts and souvenirs. These are

widely available in Bangkok at markets such as Chatuchak and shops like Narayana Phand (see p39). Items on offer include clothes and bags made of silk and cotton, basketware, lacquerware, ceramics, wall hangings, and woodcarvings.

8 Jewelry and Gems

Attractive Thai gold and silver jewelry is of a high standard. The small but upscale Peninsula Plaza is best for jewelry shops. Thailand is also known for its gems, particularly rubies and sapphires. However, beware of gem scams (see p109).
🔹 Peninsula Plaza: 153 Ratchadamri Road • Map Q3 • (02) 253 9791 • Open 10am–8pm daily

9 Tailored Clothes

Cheap cloth and labor make tailor-made clothes an attractive proposition to Westerners. But cheap prices can mean inferior quality. Go to reputed tailors such as Tailor on Ten. They can copy a garment or a picture of the style you want and measure you to get the perfect fit.
🔹 Tailor on Ten: Sukhumvit Soi 8 • Map T6 • (084) 877 1543

10 Packing and Shipping

Many shops offer packing and shipping services. Post offices also offer efficient packing services.

Left **Angelini's Restaurant, Shangri-La Hotel** Right **Ibrik Resort**

Top 10 Accommodation and Dining Tips

1 Booking a Hotel
It is a good idea to book your hotel room well in advance of your visit, especially if the hotel in question is highly rated, and even more so during the high season (Nov–Feb) or during major festivals. However, only a few budget hotels and guesthouses will accept advance booking; for most, it is simply a matter of first come, first served.

2 Seasonal Rates
Hotel rates hit a peak during the cool season (Nov–Feb), when many establishments operate at full occupancy. For the rest of the year, it is worth enquiring about discounts, especially if you plan to stay several nights. Some budget hotels and guesthouses also offer competitive monthly rates.

3 Top-End Hotels
In Bangkok, five-star accommodation can cost as little as a mid-range hotel in Europe or the US. For your money, you can expect a large room with a decent view, luxurious furnishings and decor, plenty of on-site restaurants and bars, and attentive service (see pp112–13).

4 Mid-Range Hotels
Mid-range hotels offer all the basic comforts like air-conditioned rooms, bathrooms with hot water, and TVs, but with-out the luxurious touches and elegance of top-end hotels. Within this price range, it is worth checking out the rapidly growing number of boutique hotels that offer a more personal touch and unique character, often missing even in top-end hotels (see pp114–15).

5 Budget Hotels
With its cheap cost of living, Bangkok attracts a constant stream of budget tourists, mostly to Khao San Road, the "backpackers' ghetto." A typical budget room will be small, often without windows, with a bed, a fan, paper-thin walls, and shared-bathroom facilities (see pp116–17).

6 When to Eat
You can eat any time of the day in Bangkok. Though most Thais have breakfast, lunch, and dinner at regular hours, portions are not large so they often nibble on other snacks throughout the day. Since most Thai food has a good nutritional balance, such indulgence is not fattening.

7 Where to Eat
Eat in fancy restau-rants, at street stalls, and everywhere in between. While only a few restaurants are expensive, some of Bangkok's best food can be found at street stalls, so be adventurous and try everything.

8 How to Eat
Thai food is eaten with a spoon and fork. Use the fork to push rice and other food onto the spoon, and the spoon to carry it to your mouth. Since all Thai food preparation calls for bite-sized pieces of meat or vegetables, a knife is unnecessary. Most noodle dishes are eaten with chopsticks and a soup spoon. When eating with a group of people, take a spoonful at a time from communal dishes, eat it mixed with the rice on your plate, and then go back for more.

9 Dress Code
Thais wear whatever they feel like when they eat out. The only exceptions to this are a few restaurants which encourage a sense of exclusivity by insisting on "smart casual" dress. This means that sandals, shorts, and sleeveless shirts are not permitted, but patrons need not wear a jacket or tie.

10 Tipping
The concept of tipping, once alien to Thais, has been happily embraced by restaurant staff. This is especially true for tourist areas. The 10 percent rule that people follow in the West does not apply in Bangkok. Leave whatever you think the staff deserve; every *baht* will be appreciated.

Left **Four Seasons Hotel** Center **Oriental Hotel** Right **Shangri-La Hotel**

Luxury Hotels

1 Oriental Hotel
This historic hotel (see p79) has hosted eminent guests for over a century and has often been voted as one of the best places to stay in the world for its superb facilities, exceptional views, and personalized service. ◊ 48 Oriental Avenue • Map M5 • (02) 659 9000 • www.mandarinoriental.com/bangkok • BBBBB

2 Four Seasons Hotel
Luxurious rooms, impeccable service, and fine restaurants make this one of Bangkok's best hotels. It is in an excellent location with views over the green expanse of the Royal Bangkok Sports Club. ◊ 155 Ratchadamri Road • Map Q3 • (02) 236 7777 • www.fourseasons.com • BBBBB

3 Sukhothai Hotel
The Sukhothai Hotel combines traditional Thai architecture with modern conveniences. Surrounded by lush gardens and pools, the hotel has luxurious rooms, three excellent restaurants, and a pool terrace café. ◊ 13/3 South Sathorn Road • Map Q5 • (02) 344 8888 • www.sukhothaihotel.com • BBBBB

4 Conrad Hotel
Designed in contemporary Thai style with lavish use of silk and wood, Conrad Hotel has lovely views over Lumphini Park (see p80). It has a central location and its restaurants and bars are among the best in town. ◊ All Seasons Place, Withayu Road • Map R4 • (02) 690 9999 • www.conradhotels.com • BBBBB

5 Anantara Bangkok Riverside Resort and Spa
Built on prime property on the west bank of the Chao Phraya River, this huge complex has a splendid spa, a mini mall, many restaurants, and an exotic pool. Each room has a private balcony. ◊ 257 Charoen Nakhon Road, Thonburi • Map S6 • (02) 476 0022 • www.anantara.com • BBBBB

6 Metropolitan by COMO
Bangkok's trendiest hotel features elegant minimalist design and silk furnishings. Its two great restaurants, Nahm and Glow, and the members-only Met Bar, attract the city's top design gurus. ◊ 27 South Sathorn Road • Map Q5 • (02) 625 3322 • www.comohotels.com • BBBBB

7 Royal Orchid Sheraton
This 28-story hotel has pools and tennis courts, a fitness center and spa, restaurants serving royal Thai and Italian cuisine, and a relaxed riverside bar. ◊ 2 Captain Bush Lane • Map M4 • (02) 266 0123 • www.starwoodhotels.com/sheraton/bangkok • BBBBB

8 The Peninsula Hotel
The Peninsula has won several awards for its wave-shaped design and spacious guest rooms with fabulous views of the Chao Praya River and the city. It has a three-tiered swimming pool and restaurants featuring Pacific Rim, Thai, and Cantonese cuisine. ◊ 333 Charoen Nakhon Road • Map L6 • (02) 861 2888 • www.bangkok.peninsula.com • BBBBB

9 Shangri-La Hotel
With 800 rooms, the Shangri-La is one of Bangkok's biggest luxury hotels. It has several restaurants and bars, the excellent CHI, The Spa (see p56), a fitness center, a pool, and tennis and squash courts. ◊ 89 Soi Wat Suan Phlu, Charoen Krung Road • Map M6 • (02) 236 7777 • www.shangri-la.com • BBBBB

10 Grand Hyatt Erawan Bangkok
A grandiose entrance with towering columns leads to guest rooms with large windows, marble baths, and trendy fittings. The buffet in the Garden Lounge is a gastronomic delight. ◊ 494 Ratchadamri Road • Map Q3 • (02) 254 1234 • www.bangkok.hyatt.com • BBBBB

Unless otherwise stated, all hotels listed above accept credit cards, have en-suite bathrooms, and air-conditioning

Price Categories

For a standard, double room per night (with breakfast if included), taxes, and extra charges.

B under B500
BB B500–1,000
BBB B1,000–2,000
BBBB B2,000–4,000
BBBBB over B4,000

Sheraton Grande Sukhumvitl

🔟 Business Hotels

1 InterContinental Hotel

Towering above Chit Lom's business district, this 37-story hotel is perfect for business travelers. Huge rooms offer great views from the double-glazed, soundproofed windows. All rooms have high-speed Internet access. ✆ 973 Ploenchit Road • Map Q2 • (02) 656 0444 • www.intercontinental. com • BBBBB

2 Lebua at State Tower

This distinctive skyscraper with its golden dome is one of Bangkok's icons. It is also home to Sirocco and Breeze (see p85), two of the city's top dining venues, as well as the stunning Sky Bar (see p86). ✆ 1055 Silom Road • Map M6 • (02) 624 9999 • www. lebua.com • BBBBB

3 Banyan Tree Hotel

Designed with relaxation in mind, this slender skyscraper features one of Bangkok's top spas, the Banyan Tree Spa (see p56). The aptly named Vertigo Restaurant is on the 61st floor. ✆ Thai Wah II Building, 21/100 South Sathorn Road • Map Q5 • (02) 679 1200 • www.banyantree.com • BBBBB

4 Dusit Thani Hotel

One of Bangkok's biggest and oldest hotels, Dusit Thani has a perfect location right opposite Lumphini Park (see p80). Its rooms are lavishly decorated with teak furnishings and silk trimmings. ✆ 946 Rama IV Road • Map Q5 • (02) 236 9999 • www.dusit.com • BBBBB

5 Crowne Plaza Hotel

This centrally located hotel provides a welcome retreat from the hectic streets outside. Its restaurants offer a choice of Thai, Japanese, Chinese, and international cuisine. ✆ 952 Rama IV Road • Map Q5 • (02) 632 9000 • www.crowneplaza bkk.com • BBBBB

6 Sheraton Grande Sukhumvit

Among Bangkok's best business hotels, the Sheraton Grande offers modern elegance with state-of-the-art facilities. Its business center is open 24 hours and a foot bridge connects the hotel directly to the Asoke Skytrain station. ✆ 250 Sukhumvit Road • Map T6 • (02) 649 8888 • www. sheratongrandesukhumvit. com • BBBBB

7 Westin Grande Sukhumvit

The guest rooms and suites at the Westin Grande are designed with executive travelers in mind, complete with soft beds and flat-screen TVs. The Vareena Spa and the Horizons Sky Lounge have panoramic views. ✆ 259 Sukhumvit Road • Map T6 • (02) 207 8000 • www.westin.com/ bangkok • BBBBB

8 Majestic Grande Sukhumvit

Conveniently located, this opulent hotel offers a good range of facilities for business guests, including generous desk space in rooms and a translation service in the business center. ✆ 12 Sukhumvit Soi 2 • Map R3 • (02) 262 2999 • www. majesticgrande.com • BBBBB

9 Millennium Hilton Hotel

With a sleek design, this 32-story super-modern hotel offers great views of the Chao Phraya River. Facilities include a variety of restaurants, ten stylish boardrooms, an executive lounge, and a revolving bar on the top floor. ✆ 123 Charoennakorn Road 2 • Map L5 • (02) 442 2000 • www.hilton.co.uk/bangkok • BBBBB

10 Novotel Bangkok

The hotel's 400 rooms come with everything, from king-size beds and bathtubs to high-speed Internet access and free tea- and coffee-making machines. It also houses Concept CM² (see p87), an entertainment hot spot. ✆ Soi 6, Siam Square • Map P2 • (02) 209 8888 • www.novotelbkk.com • BBBBB

Left **Siam@Siam** Center **Triple Two Silom** Right **Ibrik Resort**

Boutique Hotels

Luxx Hotel
1 The minimalist appearance of the suites and compact rooms will appeal to the young, hip, and trendy, and the location, just a few steps from the shops and nightlife of Silom Road, could not be better.
Ⓢ *6/11 Decho Road • Map N5 • (02) 635 8800 • www. staywithluxx.com • BBBB*

Siam@Siam
2 This futuristic hotel and spa has an excellent location near the shops of Siam Square. The rooms are artistically appointed and feature high ceilings and large, clear bay windows. All rooms have high-speed Internet access and there are also business and fitness centers and an in-house spa. Ⓢ *865 Rama I Road • Map N2 • (02) 217 3000 • www.siamatsiam. com • BBBBB*

Shanghai Mansion
3 Located in the heart of Chinatown, this chic and unusual hotel has just over 50 smallish rooms that are fitted with four-poster beds and are painted in vibrant colors, though some lack windows. There is a restaurant, massage/spa facilities, and a shuttle *tuk-tuk* service for guests. The management can arrange sightseeing tours. Ⓢ *479–81 Yaowarat Road • Map L3 • (02) 221 2121 • www.shanghai mansion.com • BBBB*

S2S Boutique Resort
4 Though located in the crowded district of Pratunam, this hotel is surrounded by a garden with a small waterfall. The rooms are painted in muted tones, with solid, comfortable furnishings, and pleasant views of the garden. Ⓢ *21/1 Soi Ratchataphan, Ratchaparop Road • Map T5 • (02) 642 4646 • www.s2sbangkok hotel.com • BBBB*

Siam Heritage
5 The rooms of this hotel are decorated and furnished in Northern and Central Thai style, with polished wood floors and antique furnishings. Services include a business center, a spa, and a terrace restaurant. Ⓢ *115/1 Surawong Road • Map P5 • (02) 353 6101 • www.thesiamheritage. com • BBBBB*

Silom Serene
6 With sumptuously furnished and decorated rooms, ranging from small, deluxe quarters to large, cozy suites, this small hotel near the heart of Silom's shops and nightlife, treats its guests like royalty. Facilities include an attractive pool and Jacuzzi, a stylish business center, and the Ormthong restaurant serving international and Thai cuisine. Ⓢ *7 Soi Pipat, Silom Road • Map P5 • (02) 636 6599 • www. silom-serene.com • BBBBB*

Triple Two Silom
7 The marble floors, woven rugs, and old photographs give this hotel a homely feel. It has a business center and restaurant. Ⓢ *222 Silom Road • Map N5 • (02) 627 2222 • www.tripletwosilom. com • BBBBB*

Chakrabongse Villas
8 Located on the Chao Phraya River, near Wat Pho and with amazing views of Wat Arun, this stunning small hotel comprises just six individual suites set in lush tropical gardens with a riverside dining terrace. Ⓢ *396 Maharaj Road, Tatien • Map T6 • (02) 222 1290 • www.thaivillas.com • BBBBB*

Arun Residence
9 This charming small hotel stands right beside the Chao Phraya River looking across Wat Arun, up a short Thai-Chinese shophouse lane, just across from Wat Pho. Ⓢ *36–38 Soi Pratu Nokyung, Maharat Road • Map C3 • (02) 221 9158 • www.arun residence.com • BBBBB*

Ibrik Resort
10 Arguably the world's smallest resort, the Ibrik has just three airy and welcoming rooms in an idyllic location beside the Chao Phraya River. Ⓢ *256 Soi Wat Rakhang, Arunamarin Road • Map B3 • (02) 848 9220 • www. ibrikresort.com • BBBB*

Unless otherwise stated, all hotels listed above accept credit cards, have en-suite bathrooms, and air-conditioning

Above **Wall Street Inn**

Price Categories

For a standard, double room per night (with breakfast if included), taxes, and extra charges.

B	under B500
BB	B500–1,000
BBB	B1,000–2,000
BBBB	B2,000–4,000
BBBBB	over B4,000

Mid-Range Hotels

1 Prince Palace Hotel
The hotel is named for a son of Rama V (*see p34*) who once lived on its site. The rooms are traditionally furnished and smartly decorated. Located near the Old City, it also has a pool and a fitness center. ◊ *488/800 Bo Bae Tower, Damrongrak Road • Map F3 • (02) 628 1111 • www. princepalace.co.th • BBBB*

2 Bhiman Inn
This inn has small but smart and well-equipped rooms in the heart of the backpacker district. There is also a small swimming pool and a kitchen that turns out international and Thai dishes. ◊ *55 Phra Sumen Road • Map C2 • (02) 282 6171–5 • www.bhimaninn.com • BBB*

3 Ma Hotel
The rooms in this downtown hotel provide adequate comforts, including air-conditioning, satellite TV, and minibar, at very reasonable rates, particularly for Internet bookings. Facilities include a fitness room, a massage parlor, and an indoor swimming pool. ◊ *412 Surawong Road • Map M5 • (02) 234 5070–88 • www.mahotel bangkok.com • BBB*

4 The Rose Hotel
Close to much of the Silom area's great shopping and nightlife, the Rose offers comfortable, quiet rooms in contemporary Asian style. It has a swimming pool, an excellent restaurant, a gym, and a sauna. ◊ *118 Surawong Road • Map N4 • (02) 266 8268 • www.rosehotelbkk. com • BBB*

5 Silom Village Inn
Built to recreate the atmosphere of a traditional Thai village in the heart of Bangkok's most famous nightlife district, this small hotel offers superior and deluxe rooms as well as suites at affordable rates. The hotel also hosts nightly cultural shows at the adjoining entertainment hall (*see p44*). ◊ *286 Silom Road • Map N5 • (02) 635 6810 • www.silomvillage.co.th/ hotel_silom.php • BBBB*

6 Jim's Lodge
Located near several major embassies and shopping malls, Jim's Lodge offers standard and superior rooms as well as suites. Service is very efficient and other amenities include a restaurant and rooftop jacuzzi. ◊ *125/7 Soi Ruamrudee, Ploenchit Road • Map R3 • (02) 255 3100 • www.jimslodge.com • BBBB*

7 Wall Street Inn
The smartly furnished rooms in this hotel come with comfortable beds, satellite TV, and bath tubs. There is also a business center, a coffee shop, and a massage parlor offering traditional massage and foot reflexology. ◊ *37/20–24 Surawong Road • Map P5 • (02) 233 4144 • www.wall streetinnhotel.com • BBB*

8 Ambassador Hotel
One of the city's best-known hotels, the Ambassador occupies a prime site just off Sukhumvit Road. With everything a visitor might require, such as tailors, gift shops, a business center, laundry, and beauty salon all on site, the Ambassador is like a town in itself. ◊ *171 Sukhumvit Soi 11 • Map T6 • (02) 254 0444 • www. amtel.co.th • BBB*

9 Federal Hotel
This hotel offers good value in its handful of small rooms set in a quiet compound. The swimming pool and café (open 24 hours) are added attractions. ◊ *27 Sukhumvit Soi 11 • Map T6 • (02) 253 0175 • www. federalbangkok.com • BBB*

10 Atlanta Hotel
This classic 1950s hotel is Bangkok's self-proclaimed bastion of culturally sensitive tourism. It has a decent restaurant and two swimming pools – one for adults and one for kids. ◊ *78 Sukhumvit Soi 2 • Map T6 • (02) 252 6069 • www.theatlanta hotelbangkok.com • BBB*

Left **Suk 11** Center **Wendy House** Right **A-One Inn**

Budget Hotels

Suk 11

One of Bangkok's best budget deals for its great location and quirky design, Suk 11 is so popular that potential guests are asked to book at least three days in advance. Rooms are small and basic, but all come with air-conditioning. ⓢ *1/33 Sukhumvit Soi 11* • *Map T5* • *(02) 253 5927* • *www.suk11.com* • *BB*

Charlie House

Calling itself a "five-star guesthouse," Charlie House caters to individual travelers who enjoy modest living with a cordial atmosphere. Its rooms, though small, are carpeted and tastefully furnished and the staff are friendly. ⓢ *1034/36–7 Soi Saphan Khu* • *Map R5* • *(02) 679 8330–31* • *www.charliehousethailand.com* • *BB*

Bangkok City Suite

The rooms in this eight-story building are all equipped with comfortable beds, satellite TV, and air-conditioning. The hotel has a decent restaurant, Internet, and Wi-Fi access for guests. The nearest station is a 15-minute walk. ⓢ *1 Phetburi Road* • *Map G3* • *(02) 613 7277* • *www.bangkoksuite.com* • *BB*

A-One Inn

Tucked just around the corner from Siam Square, the shoppers' paradise, this upscale guesthouse has basic but clean rooms. The staff are friendly, there is Internet access, and it is only a few steps from the National Stadium Skytrain. ⓢ *25/13 Soi Kasemsan 1, Rama I Road* • *Map P2* • *(02) 215 3029* • *www.aoneinn.com* • *BB*

Wendy House

This is another budget option near Siam Square, where the staff are friendly and enthusiastic. The small rooms, which are equipped with coffee- and tea-making facilities and fridges, are kept spotlessly clean. Rates include breakfast. ⓢ *36/2 Soi Kasemsan 1, Rama I Road* • *Map P2* • *(02) 214 1149* • *www.wendyguesthouse.com* • *BBB*

Baan Hualampong

This guesthouse has singles, doubles, and group rooms at very cheap rates. Bathroom facilities are shared, and there are communal kitchens, laundry facilities, and lounges with Internet access. ⓢ *336/20 Soi Chalong Krung, Rama IV Road* • *Map M4* • *(02) 639 8054* • *www.baanhualampong.com* • *BB*

New Empire Hotel

This hotel has smart, carpeted rooms with air-conditioning, satellite TV, and bathrooms with hot water at reasonable prices. The rooms on the upper floors have great views of the river. ⓢ *572 Yaowarat Road* • *Map D5* • *(02) 234 6990–96* • *www.newempirehotel.com* • *BB*

Riverview Guesthouse

Located in a backstreet alley beside the San Jao Sien Khong temple, this guesthouse has cheap and functional rooms and a good view of the Chao Phraya River from the upper floors. ⓢ *768 Songwad Road* • *Map L4* • *(02) 235 8501* • *www.riverviewbkk.com* • *BB*

Sala Thai Daily Mansion

At the end of a winding lane is this quiet refuge with small, clean rooms and shared bathrooms. There is a rooftop garden, and a communal sitting area. The staff are friendly but do not admit late-night non-residents. The rooms are so cheap that many guests rent them by the month. ⓢ *15 Soi Saphan Khu* • *Map R6* • *(02) 287 1436* • *B*

Woodlands Inn

This hotel is located next to the main post office. It offers small but clean rooms with air-conditioning, satellite TV, and bathrooms with hot water. The staff are very helpful and there is a good Indian restaurant. ⓢ *1158/5–7 Charoen Krung Soi 32* • *Map M5* • *(02) 235 3894* • *www.woodlandsinn.org* • *BB*

Budget hotels will most likely not accept credit cards and not have air-conditioning

Left **D&D Inn** Right **Buddy Lodge**

Khao San Road Accommodations

Buddy Lodge
A gem of a guesthouse that proves the backpacker's enclave of Khao San Road is going upscale. Very popular despite its high rates, the lodge features smart rooms with polished floors and balconies; those at the top are quieter. There is also a rooftop pool and even a spa with rates that appeal to budget travelers. ✆ 265 Khao San Road • Map C3 • (02) 629 4477 • www.buddylodge.com • BBBB

D&D Inn
This pleasant guesthouse has small rooms with all the basic amenities plus Internet access, a rooftop pool, a beauty salon, and a well-appointed restaurant. A great place to meet people. ✆ 68–70 Khao San Road • Map C3 • (02) 629 0526 • www.khaosanby.com • BBB

Viengtai Hotel
This hotel has a range of rooms at varying prices. Rates are not cheap but the rooms are a decent size and comfor-tably furnished. There is a swimming pool, a restaurant, and seminar rooms. ✆ 42 Soi Ram Buttri • Map C3 • (02) 280 5434–45 • www.viengtai.co.th • BBBB

Lamphu House
The rooms in this classic Khao San guest-house range from those that are windowless, fan-cooled, with shared baths, to ones with air-conditioning, private baths, and a balcony with a garden view. ✆ 75 Soi Ram Buttri • Map C3 • (02) 629 5861–2 • www.lamphuhouse.com • BB

New Siam 2
This modern budget hotel offers peace and privacy near the banks of the Chao Phraya River. Rooms are well-equipped with in-room safes and private bathrooms, while air conditioning costs extra. There is a small swimming pool. ✆ 50 Trok Rong Mai • Map C2 • (02) 282 2795 • www.newsiam.net • BB

Old Bangkok Inn
Styling itself as a "boutique inn," this non-smoking establishment offers five types of rooms, named after plants and flowers. Each is fitted with teak furnishings, DVD players, and computer terminals with Internet access. The rooms are of varying size and have distinctive decor. ✆ 609 Phra Sumen Road • Map D3 • (02) 629 1787 • www.oldbangkokinn.com • BBBB

Shanti Lodge
This welcoming hostel describes itself as an "oasis for backpackers" – a good summary of the quiet location, friendly ambience, and reasonable prices for rooms. Only some rooms have air-conditioning and en-suite bathrooms. ✆ 37 Sri Ayutthaya Soi 16 • Map D1 • (02) 281 2497 • www.shantilodge.com • BB

New World City Hotel
This centrally located hotel offers good-sized rooms with air-conditioning, private bathroom, fridge, and balcony. Other facilities include a restaurant, fitness room, massage service, Internet access, laundry, and babysitting service. ✆ Samsen Road Soi 2 • Map C2 • (02) 281 5596 • www.newworldcityhotel.com • BBB

Sawasdee Banglumpoo Inn
One of the seven hotels run by the Sawasdee chain, which offers small rooms with private bathrooms, air-conditioning, satellite TV, Internet access, and an on-site restaurant. There are discounted rates for online bookings. ✆ 162 Khao San Road • Map C3 • (02) 282 3748 • www.sawasdeebanglumpooinn.com • BB

Rambuttri Village Inn
The smart but simply furnished rooms here have air-conditioning and private bathrooms. There is a pool on the roof. ✆ 95 Soi Ram Bhuttri • Map C3 • (02) 282 9162 • www.khaosan-hotels.com • BB

Streetsmart

General Index

Acknowledgments

The Author
Ron Emmons is a Thailand-based British writer and photographer whose work has appeared in a wide variety of international magazines and guidebooks, including the *DK Eyewitness Travel Guide to Malaysia and Singapore*.

Main Photographer Alex Robinson
Additional Photography
Philip Blenkinsop, Stuart Isett
Fact Checker Keith Mundy

At DK INDIA
Managing Editor Aruna Ghose
Design Manager Priyanka Thakur
Project Editor Souvik Mukherjee
Project Designers Mathew Kurien, Stuti Tiwari Bhatia
Senior Cartographer Suresh Kumar
Cartographer Jasneet Kaur Arora
Illustrator Arun Pottirayil
Senior Picture Researcher Taiyaba Khatoon
Picture Researcher Sumita Khatwani
Picture Research Assistance
Shweta Andrews
Indexer & Proofreader Pooja Kumari
Senior DTP Designer Vinod Harish

At DK LONDON
Publisher Douglas Amrine
List Manager Christine Stroyan
Editor Ros Walford
Design Manager Mabel Chan
Senior Designer Paul Jackson
Senior Cartographic Editor Casper Morris
Picture Research Ellen Root
DTP Designer Natasha Lu
DK Picture Library Romaine Werblow
Production Inderjit Bhullar
Revisions Team Claire Baranowski, Marta Bescos, CPA Media/David Henley, Fay Franklin, Laura Jones, Bharti Karakoti, Nicola Malone, James Marshall, Catherine Palmi, Rada Radojicic, Mick Shippen, Susana Smith, Conrad Van Dyk

Picture Credits
The publishers would like to thank the following for their assistance and kind permission to photograph at their establishments:

Angelini Restaurant at Shangri-La Hotel; Bangkok's Children Discovery Museum; Bangkok Dolls Museum; Bangkok Planetaruim; Suchana Sasivongbhakdi and Hannah Cadwallader at Banyan Tree Spa; The Barbican; The Black Swan Pub; The Brown Sugar; Buddy Lodge Hotel; The Bull's Head Pub; Cabbages and Condoms; Calypso Cabaret; Cheap Charlie's; Sureerat Sudpairak at Cy'an, The Metropolitan; D&D Inn; Deep Club; Dream World; Dusit Park; Maria Kuhn and Mayen Fok at Four Seasons Hotel; The Grand Palace and Wat Phra Kaeo; Gulliver's Traveler's Tavern; The Hard Rock Cafe; Ibrik Resort; Irish X-Change; Jamjuree Art Gallery; Supicha at The Jim Thompson House; Joe Louis Puppet Theatre; Le Lys Restaurant; Le Normandie at The Oriental; The Londoner Brew Pub; Lucifer Disko; M R Kukrit's Heritage Home; May Kaidee; Molly Malone's Irish Pub; Sompoj Sukaboon at The National Gallery; Mr. Disapong and Jarunee Incherdchai at The National Museum; National Theater; Noriega's Bar; The Oriental Hotel; The Oriental Spa at The Oriental Hotel; Patravadi Theatre; Prasart Museum; Q Bar; Riverside Terrace;

The Royal Barge National Museum; Royal Orchid Sheraton Hotel & Towers; Samutprakarn Crocodile Farm & Zoo; Saxophone Pub; Sheraton Grande Sukhumvit Hotel; Siam Discovery Center; Siam Niramit Ratchada Theatre; Siam Paragon; Siam@Siam Design Hotel & Spa; Siriraj Hospital Museum; The Spa by Mspa at The Four Seasons Hotel; Chamnong Klinthep, M.R.Sukhumbhand, Paribatra Pennapa Paisarnsupnimit at The Suan Pakkad Palace Museum; Suk 11; Tapas Cafe Spanish Bar and Restaurant; Triple Two Silom; Wall Street Inn Bangkok; Wendy House Hotel; Witch's Tavern.

Placement Key: a-above; b-below/bottom; c-centre; f-far; l-left; r-right; t-top.

The publisher would like to thank the following individuals, companies, and picture libraries for their kind permission to reproduce their photographs:

ALAMY: Pat Behnke 55clb; G.P Bowater 50-51; William Casey 96cr; Tim Graham 88tl; Jon Arnold Images Ltd 48tl; Hideo Kurihara 32-33; Mary Evans Picture Library 34tr; Melba Photo Agency 49cla; Muay Thai Stock Photography – Alan Howden 54cl; Dave Stamboulis 54tr; Steve Allen Travel Photography 14-15c; Robert Harding World Imagery/Michael Snell 44cl; Topcris 59cla; Mireille Vautier 49tr; ALINARI ARCHIVES: Fratelli Alinari Museum of the History of Photography, Florence 34tl; BANYAN TREE BANGKOK: 86tl; CORBIS: Bettmann 35br, 35tl, 35tr; Michael Freeman 29cra, 88cl; Hulton-Deutsch Collection 34cra; Kevin R. Morris 8-9c; Paul Souders 54tl; Luca I. Tettoni 9bc, 31br; Zefa/ José Fuste Raga 26tr; CPA MEDIA: Daniel Kestenholz 19tl; MASTERFILE 20-21c; Greg Stott 16-17c; PHOTOLIBRARY: Jtb Photo Communications Inc 16br; THE PLAYHOUSE THEATRE AND CABERET: 44tr; REUTERS: Claro Cortes 48cl; Chaiwat Subprasom 48tr, 55tr; SHANGRI-LA HOTEL, BANGKOK: 112tr; SHANGRI-LA HOTELS AND RESORTS: 57tc; SHERATON GRANDE SUKHUMVIT: 57cl.

All other images are © Dorling Kindersley. For further information see www.dkimages.com

Phrase Book

Thai is a tonal language and regarded by most linguists as head of a distinct language group, though it incorporates many Sanskrit words from ancient India, and some of modern English ones, too. There are five tones: mid, high, low, rising, and falling. The particular tone, or pitch, at which each syllable is pronounced determines its meaning. For instance "mâi" (falling tone) means "not," but "măi" (rising tone) is "silk." In the second column of this phrase book is a phonetic transliteration of the Thai script for English speakers, including guidance for tones in the form of accents.

Guidelines for Pronunciation

When reading the phonetics, pronounce syllables as if they form English words. For instance:

a	as in "ago"
e	as in "hen"
i	as in "thin"
o	as in "on"
u	as in "gun"
ah	as in "rather"
ai	as in "Thai"
air	as in "pair"
ao	as in "Mao Zedong"
ay	as in "day"
er	as in "enter"
ew	as in "few"
oh	as in "go"
oo	as in "boot"
OO	as in "book"
oy	as in "toy"
g	as in "give"
ng	as in "sing"

These sounds have no close equivalents in English:

eu	can be likened to a sound of disgust - the sound could be written as "errgh"
bp	a single sound between a "b" and a "p"
dt	a single sound between a "d" and a "t"

Note that when "p," "t," and "k" occur at the end of Thai words, the sound is "swallowed." Also note that many Thais use an "l" instead of an "r" sound

The Five Tones

Accents indicate the tone of each syllable.

no mark		The **mid tone** is voiced at the speaker's normal, even pitch.
á é í ó ú		The **high tone** is pitched slightly higher than the mid tone.
à è ì ò ù		The **low tone** is pitched slightly lower than the mid tone.
ǎ ě ǐ ǒ ǔ		The **rising tone** sounds like a questioning pitch, starting low and rising.
â ê î ô û		The **falling tone** sounds similar to an syllable word for emphasis.

In an Emergency

Help!	chôo-ay dôo-ay!
Fire!	fai mâi!
Where is the nearest hospital?	tâir-o-née mee rohng pa-yah-bahn yòo têe-nǎi?
Call an ambulance!	rêe-uk rót pa-yah-bahn hâi nòy!
Call a doctor!	rêe-uk mǒr hâi nòy!
Call the police!	rêe-uk dtum ròo-ut hâi nòy!

Communication Essentials

Yes	châi or krúp/kâ
No	mâi châi or mâi krúp/mâi kâ
Please can you...?	chôo-ay
Thank you	kòrp-kOOn
No, thank you	mâi ao kòrp-kOOn
Excuse me/sorry	kǒr-tôht (krúp/kâ)
Hello	sa-wùt dee (krúp/kâ)
Goodbye	lah gòrn ná
What?	a-rai?
Why?	tum-mai?
Where?	têe nǎi?
How?	yung ngai?

Useful Phrases

How are you?	kOOn sa-bai dee reu (krúp/kâ)?
Very well, thank you	sa-bai dee (krúp/kâ)
How do I get to...?	...bpai yung-ngai?
Do you speak English?	kOOn pôot pah-sǎh ung-grìt bpen mái?
Could you speak slowly?	chôo-ay pôot cháh cháh nòy dâi mái?
I can't speak Thai.	pôot pah-sǎh tai mâi bpen

Useful Words

hot	róm
cold	yen or nǎo
good	dee
bad	mâi dee
enough	por
open	bpèrt
closed	bpìt
left	sái
right	kwǎh
near	glâi
far	glai
straight ahead	yòo dtrong nâh
woman/women	pôo-yíng
man/men	pôo-chai
child/children	dèk
entrance	tahng kâo
exit	tahng òrk
toilet	hôrng náhm

Keeping in Touch

Where is the nearest public telephone?	tâir-o née mee toh-ra-sùp yòo têe-nǎi?
Can I call abroad from here?	ja toh bpai dtàhng bpra-tâyt jàhk têe-nêe dâi mái?
Hello, this is... speaking.	hello (pǒm /dee-chún)...pôot (krúp/kâ))
May I leave a message?	kǒr fàhk sǔng a-rai nòy dâi mái?

*In polite speech, Thai men add "**krúp**" at the end of each sentence; women add "**ká**" at the end of questions and "**kâ**" at the end of statements*

would like to speak to...	kŏr pôot gùp khun ... nòy (krúp/kà)
local call	toh-ra-sùp pai nai tórng tìn
phone card	but toh-ra-sùp

Shopping

How much does this cost?	nêe rah-kah tâo-rài?
I would like...	dtôrng-gahn...
Do you have?	mee...mái?
I am just looking	chom doo tâo-nún
Do you take credit cards/travelers' checks?	rub but cray-dìt/ chék dern tang mái?
What time do you open/close?	bpèrt/bpìt gèe mohng?
Can you ship this overseas?	sóng kŏng nee bpai dtàhng bpra-tâyt dâi mái?
Could you lower the price a bit?	lót rah-kah nòy dâi mái?
How about...baht?	...bàht dâi mái?
That's a little expensive.	pairng bpai nòy
Will you go for...baht?	...bàht bpai mái?
I'll settle for...baht.	...bàht gôr láir-o-gun
cheap	tòok
expensive	pairng
Does it come in other colors?	mee sĕe èun èek mái?
black	sĕe dum
blue	sĕe núm ngern
green	sĕe kĕe-o
red	sĕe dairng
white	sĕe kăo
yellow	sĕe lĕu-ung
gold	torng
silver	ngern
Thai silk	păh-măi tai
ladies' wear	sêu-păh sa-dtree
bookstore	ráhn kăi núng-sĕu
department store	hâhng
pharmacy	ráhn kăi yah
market	dta-làht
newsstand	ráhn kăi núng-sĕu pim
shoe shop	ráhn kăi rorng táo
supermarket	sÓOp-bpêr-mah-gèt
tailor	ráhn dtùt sêu-a

Staying in a Hotel

Do you have a vacant room?	mee hôrng wâhng mái?
air-conditioned room	hôrng air
I have a reservation.	jorng hôrng wái láir-o
I'd like a room for one night/three nights.	(pŏm/dee-chún) ja púk yòo keun nèung/ săhm keun
What is the charge per night?	kâh hôrng wun la tâo-rài?
I don't know yet how long I'll stay	mâi sâhp wâh ja yòo nahn tâo-rài
May I see the room first please?	kŏr doo hôrng gòrn dâi mái?
May I leave some things in the safe?	kŏr fàhk kŏrng wái nai dtôo sáyf dâi mái?
Will you spray some mosquito repellent, please?	chôo-ay chèet yah gun yOOng hâi nòy dâi mâi?

double/twin room	hôrng kôo
single room	hôrng dèe-o
bedroom	hôrng norn
bill	bin
fan	pút lom
hotel	rohng-rairm
key	gOOn-jair
manager	pôo-jùt-gahn
mosquito screen	mÓOng lôo-ut
shower	fúk boo-a
swimming pool	sá wâi náhm

Sightseeing

travel agent	bor-ri sùt num tée-o
tourist office	sŭm-núk ngahn gahn tôrng tée-o
tourist police	dtum-ròo-ut tôrng tée-o
beach	hâht or chai-hâht
cliff	nâh păh
festival	ngahn órk ráhn
hill/mountain	kăo
historical park	ÒO-ta-yahn-bpra wùt sàht
island (koh)	gòr
lake	ta-lay sáhp
museum	pí-pít-ta-pun
national park	ÒO-ta yahn háirng châht
palace	wang
park/garden	sŏo-un
river	mâir náhm
ruins	boh-rahn sa-tăhn
temple (wat)	wút
Thai boxing	moo-ay tai
Thai massage	nôo-ut
trekking	gahn dern tahng táo
waterfall	náhm dtòk
zoo	sŏo-un sàt

Transportation

When does the train for...leave?	rót fai bpai...òrk meu-rài?
How long does it take to get to...?	chái way-lah nahn tâo-rài bpai tĕung tée...?
A ticket to... please.	kŏr dtŏo-a bpai... nòy (krúp/kà)
Which platform for the...train?	rót fai bpai..yòo chahn cha-lah năi?
What station is this?	tèe nêe sa-tăhn-nee a-rai?
I'd like to reserve a seat, please.	kŏr jorng têe nùng
Where is the bus station?	sa-tăhn-nee rót may yòo têe-năi?
Which buses go to...?	rót may sâi năi bpai...?
What times does the bus for...leave?	rót may bpai...òrk gèe mohng?
Would you tell me when we get to...?	tĕung...láir-o chôo- ay bòrk dôo-ay?
Is it far?	glai mái?
ticket	dtŏo-a
air-conditioned bus	rót bprùp ah-gàht
airport	sa-năhm bin
tour bus	rót too-a
train	rót fai
bus station	sa-tăhn-nee rót may
moped	rót mor-dter-sai
bicycle	rót jùk-gra-yahn
taxi	táirk-sêe

Eating Out

A table for two please.	kŏr dtó sŭm-rúp sŏrng kon
May I see the menu?	kŏr doo may-noo nòy?
Do you have...?	mee...mái?
I'd like...	kŏr...
I didn't order this.	nêe mâi dâi sùng (krúp/kâ)
Is it spicy?	pèt mái?
Not too spicy, ok?	mâi ao pèt mâhk na
I can eat Thai food.	tahn ah-hăhn tai bpen
May I have a glass of water, please.	kŏr núm kăirng bplào gâir-o nèung
Waiter/waitress!	kOOn (krúp/kâ)
The check, please.	kŏr bin nòy (krúp/kâ)
bottle	kòo-ut
chopsticks	dta-gèe-up
drink(s)	krêu-ung dèum
fork	sôrm
glass	gâir-o
menu	may-noo
spoon	chórn

Menu Decoder

nòr mái	bamboo shoots
glôoy-ay	banana
néu-a woo-a	beef
bee-a	beer
dtôm	boiled
yâhng	char-grilled
gài	chicken
prík	chili
gah-fair	coffee
bpoo	crab
mèe gròrp	crispy noodles
gŏo-ay dtěe-o hâirng	dry noodles
bpèt	duck
tÓO-ree-un	durian
kài	egg
bplah	fish
kĭng	ginger
núm kăirng bplào	iced water
ka-nŎOn	jackfruit
mâir-kŏhng	Mekong Whisky
hèt	mushroom
gŏo-ay dtěe-o-náhm	noodle soup
ma-la-gor	papaya
sùp-bpa-rót	pineapple
néu-a-mŏo	pork
kâo	rice
gŏo-ay dtěe-o	rice noodles
gÔOng	shrimp
núm sĕe éw	soup
ah-hăhn wăhng	soy sauce
pùk ka-náh	spring greens
kâo-nĕe-o	sticky rice
kâo pôht	sweet corn
núm chah	tea
pùk	vegetables
náhm	water

Health

I do not feel well	róa-sèuk mâi sa-bai
It hurts here.	jèp dtrong nêe
I have a fever.	dtoo-a-rórn bpen kâi
sore throat	jèp kor
stomach ache	bpòo-ut tórng
vomit	ah-jee-un
asthma	rôhk hèut ai
cough	ai
diabetes	rôhk bao wăhn
diarrhea	tórng sĕe-a
dizzy	wee-un hŏo-a
dysentry	rôhk bìt
fever	kâi
headache	bpòo-ut hŏo-a
aspirin	air-sa-bprin or yah-gâir kâi
doctor	mŏr
dentist	tun-dta-pâirt or mŏr fun
hospital	rohng pa-yah-bahn
injection	chèet yah
medicine	yah
prescription	bai sùng yah
How many tablets do I take?	dtôhng gin yah gèe mét dtòr krúng
I'm allergic to...	(pŏm/dee-chún) páir...

Numbers

0	sŏon
1	nèung
2	sŏrng
3	săhm
4	sèe
5	hâh
6	hòk
7	jèt
8	bpàirt
9	gâo
10	sìp
11	sìp-èt
12	sìp-sŏrng
13	sìp-săhm
14	sìp-sèe
15	sìp-hâh
16	sìp-hòk
17	sìp-jèt
18	sìp-bpàirt
19	sìp-gâo
20	yêe-sìp
30	săhm-sìp
40	sèe-sìp
50	hâh-sìp
60	hòk-sìp
70	jèt-sìp
80	bpàirt-sìp
90	gâo-sìp
100	nèung róy
1,000	nèung pun
10,000	nèung mèun
100,000	nèung săirn

Time

one minute	nèung nah-tee
one hour	nèung chôo-a mohng
half an hour	krêung chôo-a mohng
Sunday	wun ah-tìt
Monday	wun jun
Tuesday	wun ung-kahn
Wednesday	wun pÓOt
Thursday	wun pa-réu-hùt
Friday	wun sÒOk
Saturday	wun săo
a day	neung wun
a week	nèung ah-tìt
a weekend	sÒOt sùp-pah-dah
a month	nèung deu-un
a year	nèung bpee